Contents

Introduction

Live chat is like a cross between email and a radio phone-in.

The Internet is both exhilarating and alarming. It is exciting because anything is possible in what is, effectively, the whole interconnected world. And it is frightening because we do not know how it will change the way we think, work, and interact.

We do know that we have got to engage with it—or get left behind. Dot-coms are everywhere; almost everyone now has email. In addition, radio and television programmes offer 'live chat' where people continue to debate issues and offer instant feedback. Selected comments sent online sometimes appear later in the programme.

Increasingly, we see online writing interacting with business and with leisure. It has become the modern form of letter writing. It is so easy to communicate across continents that people—who perhaps did not write regularly before—are now finding they correspond daily with friends, relations, business contacts, and strangers.

So perhaps it's time to reassess the way we write. We now have two parallel cultures in everyday writing: the official, school-taught business style and the personal, chat-mail mode that millions of people are co-inventing. Where will it lead?

The fact is, we read differently from screens and must write differently for them. This book looks at various aspects of that difference. In particular:

■ Screen resolutions vary greatly and many are tiring on the eyes, so **concise writing** helps readers get quickly to the point.

■ Design conventions are not standardized, so **clear headings** help users find what they want.

**THE PARK
LEARNING CENTRE**
The Park, Cheltenham
Gloucestershire GL50 2RH
Telephone: 01242 714333

UNIVERSITY OF
GLOUCESTERSHIRE
at Cheltenham and Gloucester

NORMAL LOAN

654 4/2011

One Step Ahead ...

The *One Step Ahead* series is for all those who want and need to communicate more effectively in a range of real-life situations. Each title provides up-to-date practical guidance, tips, and the language tools to enhance your writing and speaking.

Series Editor: John Seely

Titles in the series

Editing and Revising Texts	Jo Billingham
Essays and Dissertations	Chris Mounsey
Organizing and Participating in Meetings	Judith Leigh
Publicity, Newsletters, and Press Releases	Alison Baverstock
Punctuation	Robert Allen
Spelling	Robert Allen
Words	John Seely
Writing for the Internet	Jane Dorner
Writing Reports	John Seely

Acknowledgements

Many thanks to Beatrice Baumgartner-Cohen for drawing the cartoons.
Many thanks to Tom Campbell of New Media Knowledge and to Richard Boulton for checking the accuracy of the text.

Editorial note: websites are frequently updated. All websites were up to date at time of publishing.

Writing for the Internet

Jane Dorner

Cartoons by Beatrice Baumgartner-Cohen

OXFORD
UNIVERSITY PRESS

OXFORD UNIVERSITY PRESS

Great Clarendon Street, Oxford OX2 6DP

Oxford University Press is a department of the University of Oxford.
It furthers the University's objective of excellence in research, scholarship,
and education by publishing worldwide in
Oxford New York
Auckland Bangkok Buenos Aires Cape Town Chennai
Dar es Salaam Delhi Hong Kong Istanbul Karachi Kolkata
Kuala Lumpur Madrid Melbourne Mexico City Mumbai Nairobi
São Paulo Shanghai Singapore Taipei Tokyo Toronto
with an associated company in Berlin

Oxford is a registered trade mark of Oxford University Press
in the UK and in certain other countries

Published in the United States
by Oxford University Press Inc., New York

British Library Cataloguing in Publication Data
Data available

Library of Congress Cataloging in Publication Data
Data available

ISBN 0-19-866285-8

10 9 8 7 6 5 4 3 2 1

Design and typesetting by David Seabourne
Printed in Spain by Bookprint S.L., Barcelona

- People cannot see the whole site (as they can with a book), so writers need to find other ways of giving viewers a **sense of position**—where they are and where they can go next.

- The web has a broad span—factual information as well as recreational; writers must always **think of the audience**.

You could quite rightly say, 'All writers should do these things.' The difference is that if you do not pay attention to those four issues on the web, no one will read you. On paper there are many other ways of keeping the reader engaged.

Brevity
Clarity
Positioning
Audience

These are the watchwords of writing for the web

How will this book help?

Even if you know everything in this book, it will still help. That is because there will always be someone else who wants you to post up some text that you *know* will not work on a screen. Here's the ammunition you need to persuade others that you know what you are doing.

People who write well, read a lot. They see how other people do it: what works and what does not work. In the same way, those who frequently surf (explore the web) learn from others. It is human nature, however, to be more aware of what frustrates you. Most people take good writing for granted, hardly realizing the art that goes into it.

So it is helpful to identify good practice. This book gives some pointers. In particular, it concentrates on areas of writing that everyone can improve: orderly planning of the work before it starts and self-critical revision of it once it is in draft.

Part A bases each section round a number of learning objectives and gives:
Key ideas
Techniques
Resources

Part B summarizes points made in Part A, with:
Explanations of technical terms
Useful sites and references
Good practice summaries
Legal references
Glossary

| # Reading routes

The various topics are in a logical sequence, but this book is like a web text. You do not need to read it in any particular order—look at the sections that apply to you personally. And if they do not fit your own circumstances, extract the principles that do.

None of the advice is set in stone (that is an old print term). The Internet is new and fluid. We are all finding out more about it as the technology improves; its possibilities are bounded only by the imagination of those using it.

An alternative reading order matrix might be:

Some reading routes	Beginner information	Further details
New to the web	Explanation of common terms, p. 117 Glossary, p 121	Web creation resources, pp. 115–6
Practical writing advice	Chapter 5, pp. 56ff	Checklists, pp. 105–9
Core editorial issues	Chapter 6, pp. 76ff	House style, pp. 111–12
Publishing on the web	Chapter 2, pp. 24ff	Applicable law, pp. 112–14
Thinking about users	Chapter 1, pp. 12ff Evaluating other websites, p. 38 Audience, p 42	Chapter 8, pp. 98ff Checklist p 109
Project background	Chapter 3, pp. 36ff	Chapter 7, pp. 90ff

Technical know-how

Introduction

For technical fundamentals, see pp. 117–20. There is also a glossary for other technical terms used in this book on pp. 121–3.

The Internet is just another medium, like newspapers or television. It's a little bit different and has some conventions of its own—this book explores them all.

Writers are often frightened of anything technical. If that describes you, take it slowly. Learn only as much as you absolutely must know and leave the rest to someone else. Most of us don't know how the telephone works and it doesn't stop us using it.

This book is *not* about writing code nor about understanding how the Internet works: there are books inches thick on every aspect of both those. The lone web writer, however, will need some basic knowledge in order to follow the writing advice in the rest of this book, as well as to be an effective member of a team responsible for a website.

Hypertext Hyperlink:

A highlighted word or graphic in a document that responds to a mouse click to take the user to a related piece of information on the Internet.

There may be no need to understand how web pages work, but it's as well to grasp the language of some of the mechanics because writing for the Internet involves knowing what it is, what it is good for, and why it is a new medium.

This book makes some assumptions, e.g. that readers have experimented with hyperlinking on the Internet at least once.

New writing roles

Before you start, it's as well to see where you fit in. What's your role here—have you been drawn to this book for a private purpose, because your workplace has woken up to the web and has found new tasks for you, or something else? You'll have different needs accordingly.

In the traditional world of writing—the analogue world—there are clearly defined roles of copywriters, editors, designers, printers, publishers, and readers.

In the digital world, many of these responsibilities merge. New technologies always create new functions. In films, for example, what we now know as a sound editor was once called a sound designer.

Those who write for the Internet—and for web pages specifically—are not always 'writers' in the sense in which we have understood the word so far. They may be project managers, people in marketing, or even programmers. They are knowledge stylists.

They cannot, therefore, work in isolation. Interdependency is a fact of web life. On personal websites all roles converge in one person, and that person must learn something about browsers, coding, scripting, and information design.

Browser:

Software that allows users to access and navigate the web—commonly Microsoft Explorer, Netscape, and Opera.

Where do I start?

On large corporate or institutional sites the person assigned the writing task cannot adequately fulfil the role without an understanding of what the technical and design people can do. This means that a great deal of the 'writing' happens through discussion, before anyone puts finger to keyboard.

Place in a team

Whether you are freelance or working in an office, you will probably assume one or more of the various roles and responsibilities in the chart below. On a personal site, you may do them all. When you are collaborating with others, it can be helpful to define boundaries between these roles because they are different in this new environment.

Co-ordination writer	Involved in planning and estimating; decides scope of content; handles all documents; controls timetable; coordinates with designers, technicians, and webmasters
Page writer	Responsible for parts or the whole of the writing of a website; liaises with web designers and planners
Policy editor	Makes sure all pages conform to company policy in presentation; legal requirements; accessibility; content; copyright
Copy editor (or sub-editor)	Checks that all pages are internally consistent in heading styles; house style; hyperlinking; product details; grammar; spelling; clarity
Maintenance writer	Keeps the website up to date; posts up press releases; checks links; removes or archives old material
Publicist	Publicises website via search engines, outside linking; writes press articles or company releases
Communications officer	Coordinates feedback and writes an e-zine digest to circulate by email
Code writer	Writes all code; designs style sheets; enters all HTML or XML tags; writes scripts and routines

All writers work with:

Project manager

Webmaster

Graphics designers

Programmers

1 | Communicating online

The ability to communicate online is one of the key skills needed in the new economy. What, then, do we mean by 'communicate online'? Isn't it the same as any other way in which people have conveyed thoughts and meaning to each other? Not quite. Though a facility with words is always useful, it isn't enough in itself. Every communication has to be sensitive to its context. And being online has its own conventions—whether it is on a web page, conference (or chat) 'room', email screen, or mobile text message box.

These conventions are developing with the new technologies that deliver the online opportunities. It is an exciting time: those who 'read' the new media correctly and 'write' for it with flair are the ones who will succeed.

In conventional terms, one would call that getting the right register. Register is the right tone of voice or style of writing to fit the occasion. So:

Got2go, TTFN

is customary for a text phone sign-off between friends. But the nineteenth-century equivalent might be:

Hoping this finds you in as good health as it leaves me, I remain, Sir, your humble and obedient servant.

The difference is only *partly* changed custom and practice; we are familiar rather than obedient these days. It is also that keying in 12 characters on the awkward phone keypad is easier than tapping in 105. So we've developed shorthand conventions to save time: some flippant; some already in everyday use (see box).

B2B	Business To Business	IYSS	If You Say So
BTW	By The Way	OTE	On Target Earnings
CUL8R	See You Later	OTTOMH	Off The Top Of My Head
ETA	Estimated Time of Arrival	RSVP	Please Reply
GMT	Greenwich Mean Time	TTFN	Ta Ta For Now

These abbreviations, sometimes known as 'hapspek', are only clear to those who understand them. To others, they are an irritating jumble of letters. But so too were the flourishes and flounces of handwritten script in an age when only the privileged could read.

Clear writing includes the widest possible audience by being simple and easy to understand.

Nevertheless, following fashion is an asset in developing good communication. Advertising, for example, began in turgid style with lengthy blocks of descriptive text. There was an occasional wood engraving to catch the eye. The fashion in television advertising now is to appeal almost solely to the eye. It is witty and reductive, telling whole stories in a series of pictorial situations. Audiences have become highly skilled at reading these signs.

In the same way, online communication skills involve knowing what the modern conventions are. It is productive to look at all forms of media and gather the best from them all. Then you will be able to write effectively for the Internet.

It is a new art.

Email

**Remote
communication**

Smoke signals

⬇

Jungle drums

⬇

Telegraph

⬇

Morse code

⬇

Telex

⬇

Fax

A familiar starting place for talking about writing for the Internet is email. It is such a feature of everyday life that it is hard to remember how rapidly email has spread. It is only since 1995 that it has reached a critical mass where one can expect others to have an email address, but it dates back to the 1970s.

Writing email comes before writing for the web, not just historically, but because it informs our expectations of the web. Writing clear email messages is a way of limbering up for contributing to online forums and also to writing web pages. Much that applies to the netiquette of email (see overleaf) is good practice for the web.

In its early days, email had the same level of informality as early SMS and WAP mobile phone text messaging. Lack of punctuation, disregard for capital letters after full stops, and spelling mistakes were everywhere. Many even cultivated quirky styling as expressively amusing. The assumption was people wrote while online, and telephone connection time was too expensive to waste on long messages or on getting grammar right.

Now, most offices are continuously connected to the Internet and all-day home access is growing. A messages goes as soon as you press the Send button: you cannot call it back if you have second thoughts. So best be sure you have all your second thoughts first.

Remember, although email is informal you are always sending a note to one or more other people, and all the normal 'rules' of behaviour apply. Where you only have the written word to convey every nuance of what you want to say, you need to think more carefully about it; consider where ambiguities may cause offence. It is not the same as speaking to someone face to face, where a smile may take away the sting of what is being said, or tone of voice may modify responses.

Emailed text has a large repertoire of reading-tone-of-voice signs. Like these:

;-)   wink

:-(frown

:-D   big smile

:-[)   smile with moustache

They are called 'emoticons' and have a certain limited use in place of sentence stops. In chat rooms, they convert to tiny pictures where (L) becomes ♥, etc.

Some people add email stage directions, such as <hollow laughter> to indicate that a statement is ironic, <yawn> to indicate sleepiness, or <pleading look> when you are asking someone for a favour. Clearly the conventions will settle over time, resulting in a redefinition of the way people write—in particular to what extent they use alphabetic (textual) or iconic (visual) information.

Some small offices have a policy of circulating emails to all staff for information: others prefer to limit the circulation. In either case it is easy to get overloaded. The trick is to write 'Subject' lines that contain all you need know or tell people instantly whether they need to open the email and read on.

Fire Alarm

is not as informative as

Fire practice alarm at 4 p.m. – no action required

'Email has increased rather than reduced the number of face-to-face meetings since meetings are now held to resolve disputes emerging from electronic communication.'

From a study by Dr Steven Brown of Loughborough University and Dr Geoff Lightfoot of Keele University quoted in the Electronic Telegraph, 2000.

Chat rooms

Chat sounds informal, and it is. There's almost a culture of making a virtue out of silly spelling—U rite fingz fonetickly wiv lotz of zedz—it's a way of being wry. Chat 'rooms', or virtual typing spaces, were once quite hard to get into, so those who cracked the technics of it tended to flaunt their difference by playing with language. Now that access has become very easy, some people are using chat rooms for semi-serious conferencing. So use wry or private languages where they fit, but be aware of context.

Email and chat etiquette

Mud and Moo:

Acronyms
(becoming words)
Mud = Multi-User
Domain (or
Dungeon) and
Moo = Mud Object-
Orientated. Virtual
spaces on the
Internet where
people role-play
and chat using
borrowed identities.

Email and computer conferencing, including chat rooms, forums, and the quaintly named muds and moos (see box) are Internet venues. Several people can exchange ideas using the computer to provide virtual spaces to 'meet' online. Audio and video outlets are improving, but for most individuals, this form of simultaneous exchange is still text-based.

The BBC offers three models. For a scheduled hour, frequently after a show, a politician, entertainer, or expert speaker will interactively answer questions online. Or there may be a 'Your Say' button that gives a feedback form (e.g. for *The World at One*). Editors decide what to publish online. And there are venues, like the Radio One live chat, where anyone can:

> Join us in the R1 Room to give us your views on what's hot and what's not in the worlds of R&B, Dance, Garage, Indie & more.

Live chat has 'bouncers' who make sure people are not abusive or inflammatory. The other two models operate much like email. Some good practice 'rules' for both have developed:

In live chat

 Don't!

give out personally
identifiable
information, such
as email, telephone
number, or address

 Don't!

impersonate
someone else
(friend, family, or
famous person)

Good netiquette

■ Read messages carefully before sending—in case they are offensive, or you have mis-spelled something.

■ Ask permission before forwarding or copying other people's messages—they're not yours.

■ Avoid sexist or racist language.

■ Avoid using all upper-case letters (looks as if you are SHOUTING).

■ If the message is very important, controversial, or open to misunderstanding consider a face-to-face discussion instead.

■ Select the right forum—private mail or conference. If your comment is only of interest to a limited number of people, send it to the private mailboxes.

- When joining an online group that has been in existence for some time, read through all the contributions to date (and the FAQ) to avoid asking a question or making a point that has already been made.

- Do not assume that all outrageous messages are intended to inflame opinion (they may be a clumsy attempt at humour or lack of familiarity with the medium).

- Check that you are sending the message to the right person or people—beware the Reply button, especially in listserv circulars.

- Try not to create lengthy chain debates by resending/forwarding comments and creating a string of messages.

- Take care with office circulation lists—600 people may not need to know about social events or lost coffee mugs.

Help people read messages

- Describe the content of your message clearly in the 'Subject' line and keep that subject in replies to the same conversational thread. This helps people to prioritize and to find information again later.

In email

 Do!

write single subject messages where possible

- Send short messages that can be clearly understood on their own. Do not send a short message as an attachment because it wastes time opening two emails instead of one.

 Do!

be brief and to the point

- Make the top of the message count. People will decide whether or not to read on.

- Make sure your message is written in a style that is friendly, appealing, and logical.

- Use short paragraphs. People are overwhelmed by large pieces of text. Short coherent chunks allow readers to breathe between chunks of thought and also provide relief to the eye.

Web writing

The previous pages about the need to take care in writing email messages apply also to web writing. Clarity is even more important here. Emails are private (or limited in circulation), web pages are public.

What is most important on a website: the design, the technology, or the writing? Answer: all rate equally. Yet there are several books on design and coding, and almost nothing on writing for the web. The rest of this book aims to redress that imbalance. It looks at the thinking processes, and at the nuts and bolts of how to write for screen reading.

This falls half-way between journalistic writing and writing advertising copy. Here's what the writing aims to do:

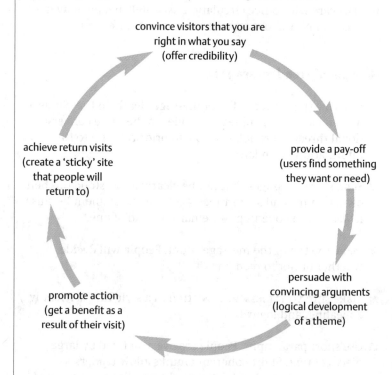

convince visitors that you are
right in what you say
(offer credibility)

provide a pay-off
(users find something
they want or need)

persuade with
convincing arguments
(logical development
of a theme)

promote action
(get a benefit as a
result of their visit)

achieve return visits
(create a 'sticky' site
that people will
return to)

All depend on language, style, and planning.

The Internet and the web

The one point about web writing it is worth emphasizing is that the terms 'Internet' and 'web' are not interchangeable.

The Internet is an umbrella term for everything that happens between the hundreds of millions of computers in homes, offices, and public buildings connected via telephone cabling. It is a net, or network, of laid lines or satellite-beamed signals with nodes (like the knots in a net) representing a sending machine and a receiving machine.

The web—also known as World Wide Web (WWW)—is a distribution mechanism and a presentation device. It delivers content, and acts as a sales medium. Sound, pictures, and graphic elements feature on websites, but the text still dominates. Perhaps 'text' is returning to its original meaning, from the Latin 'texere' (to weave) and 'textus' (a web, texture, structure). Something a spider might put together.

Areas of the Internet that depend on writing:

Email
Web pages
Newsgroups
Chat rooms

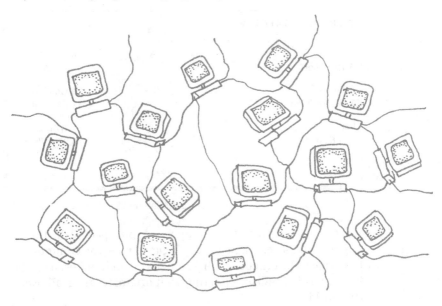

19

Dominance of the web

Bandwidth

A term used to describe how much data you can send through a connection to the Internet. The greater the bandwidth, the faster the rate of data transmission. Lack of bandwidth leads to access problems.

The web now dominates culture in the western world. But we should remember that many countries have inadequate access to it. It is not so much a lack of computers as a shortage of sufficient telephone cabling to satisfy the demand. So although people in offices, and increasingly at home, in the UK and the USA have fast access, there are still serious bandwidth constraints in the rest of the world. In parts of Africa, for example, there simply isn't enough cable capacity for everyone to be online at the same time. They have to book online access, just as we once had to book overseas telephone calls.

This means the word is still dominant on the web—people with slow or inadequate connections may have sounds and graphics turned off so that the text on the page downloads faster.

Equal access

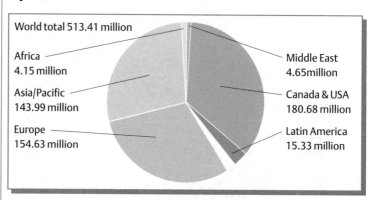

World total 513.41 million

Africa
4.15 million

Middle East
4.65 million

Asia/Pacific
143.99 million

Canada & USA
180.68 million

Europe
154.63 million

Latin America
15.33 million

Source Nua Internet Services (NUA) Aug. 2001.

It is not just the word that is important, but specifically the English language. English is the *lingua franca*—the common language of Internet exchange. Much research material on the Internet is in English, even though it originates from all over the world.

Writers, whether writing in their mother tongue or not, must be sensitive to the fact that many readers will be using a second language for all their Internet browsing.

Your voice

In the early days of the Internet, it was largely populated by young technicians who understood the (then) complications of getting connected. They imbued web writing with their own brand of informality. They decided to write the way they and their readers spoke. Perhaps that brought freshness to the web that some found appealing.

The personal voice allowed colloquialisms and jargon because it was quicker to get to the point.

That sentence could have read:

... because it was quicker to cut the crap.

The difference between the two is that they are in a different register or voice. The first is what you might say to your boss; the second to your mates. So does that mean the formality of the first sentence is right for a company website and the informality of the second for a home page?

The answer probably is that spoken English often doesn't look good written down. A phrase like 'cut the crap' draws attention to itself. Readers cannot concentrate on the meaning because some of their attention is directed on the colouring of the sentence.

That does not mean websites should be colourless, strewn with polite phrases in standard English. No one wants sanitized web language with everything blandly the same. Yet it is the case that most web writing is done to convey information quickly and easily. By all means give the readers a jolt with your message, but don't give them a jolt because the words you use puzzle or annoy them.

You write for the reader, and if your reader cannot understand you because you have chosen the wrong level of formality, or made wrong assumptions about language, then you lose that reader. On the web, the reader–user is king. The reader decides what makes sense just as they determine the reading order.

'Language always keeps pace with the social development of its users.'
David Crystal

'No one system of language is better than another.'
Ken Livingstone

Readability

Granularity – putting just the right amount of information in front of the user

Statistics show that the average person spends 8 hours a week reading books or newspapers, as opposed to 27 hours watching TV. Many of the workforce will also spend another 30 hours a week working at a computer.

Although that means we are all used to looking at screens, it does not mean we are happy reading text-based information from them. Reading from screens has so far proved to be less efficient than paper. For example, this printed page has a resolution of 1200 dots per inch—which a good comfortable definition for the eye. Screens are about 72 pixels per inch (roughly equivalent to dots). And there's some flicker. So it is more of a strain to read.

Analysts say it is 25 per cent slower and that screen resolutions will not be adequate for easy reading until 2008. There's more detail on screen resolution on page 26.

Consider how you read from screen, why you want to download some documents, whether there are any advantages in screen reading, and what disadvantages there are to reading off screen. In most online forums, the chances are people will expect to read from the screen. So that means you need to make it easy for them by being readable.

You can test how readable you are on a good word-processing package which has inbuilt readability formulae (often accessible from the spelling and grammar checker). The most useful is the Flesch, which works on a system that counts words and syllables in a sentence, crunches them up according to a formula, and then offers a score. A score of 0 means you are virtually unreadable: 100 puts you among the most readable writers. Of course, it's only a rough guide.

The figures in the box are illuminating because 'best-sellers' very often score well. A close analysis shows that today's top-selling authors use simple words (with one or two syllables) and short sentences. Jane Austen scores badly simply because her sentences have lots of subclauses.

Readability score

Barbara Cartland 89

JK Rowling 80

Terry Pratchett 78

Graham Greene 70

Jane Austen 46

Your style

Jane Austen, of course, belonged to her time. Look at how different writing technologies changed the way other authors wrote in the past (see box), and it becomes more obvious why the Internet too changes style. How many of these writers do we find it easy to read now? It isn't simply based on readability scores.

Most people have their own style, whether in the way they dress or the shape of sentences they prefer. We're affected more than we think by each other and by the technologies we use. Tapping in a text phone message is not the same as writing a postcard. Both have conventions born of the small square of space, and the forms of words or abbreviations other people use.

We've probably all used a mobile to say, 'I'm on the train' or an equivalent. Or written, 'Having a lovely time, wish you were here'. In absorbing the styles of our times, we are training the ear to make us write convincingly. A good web writer is one who writes for the present era.

Writing for the Internet is like any other form of writing. The aim is to be concise, clear, and easy to understand. That does not mean bland. But since most web-displayed prose is functional, self-indulgent individuality is out of place. Some conventions have developed over time for printed media. Now they need revisiting with the constraints of the Internet in mind. All apply in a different way to writing for reading on screen. The next chapters will develop this further.

2 Internet publishing

The Internet is a publishing medium, and it is worth emphasizing this because there is something so personal about people's own words on their own computer that it can be hard to realize they could potentially reach an audience of the world's 450 million web users (765 projected by the end of 2005). You are publicising to an audience—that's what publishing is.

When the World Wide Web began in 1990, you could count the number of users in hundreds; few realized it would have the impact it does now. As it developed during the 1990s, technical buzz and design wizardry ruled. By 2000, individuals and organizations saw that *not* having a website was like *not* having publicity handouts and a telephone number. The web became more professional as it grew up.

So it is time to take stock and realize that there are the same imperatives in electronic publishing as there are for paper. The first is that these hard-learned values about the written word remain as important now as they ever were:

Publishing style and accuracy are as important on the Internet as on paper.

- factual accuracy;

- a sieving system of readers who vet, verify, and edit the original;

- editorial accuracy (grammar, spelling, style);

- design to enhance the reading matter.

Whether the final form is on screen or on paper should not alter this process of 'gatekeeping'. The challenge for web publishing is to replicate the quality assurance we are used to in the print world.

One influencing factor that made you buy this book is a trust in OUP's standards. Your aim in writing for the web is to make sure your reader trusts *you*. Publishers traditionally provide trust by promising:

- a level of readability (through copy-editing and page design);

- ease of use (through cross-referencing, indexing, book design);

- safeguarding writers (staff writer salaries, royalties or fees, copyright protection);

- distribution (through market targeting, advertising, etc).

Of these, only the last—distribution—is actually *easier* in the online environment. The Internet is an ideal marketing tool.

The other three bear some discussion. Editing forms the subject of Chapter 6. Ease of use is dealt with in Chapters 3 and 4. The next few pages look at design, and at copyright.

Paper pages are good for:	Web pages are good for:
long attention span	quick navigation
intuitive navigation	up-to-date information
reliable information	wealth of reference
standardized display	searching
clear readable typography	combining media
good image reproduction	disabled accessibility
consistency	personalization of display
look and feel	ability to add layers of detail
Bound Optimally Ordered Knowledge (= **BOOK**)	World Enabled Business (=**WEB**)

New conventions

Body language impacts on verbal understanding. In the same way, readability is affected by design. Unfortunately, designing accurately for screen reading is almost impossible. There are so many variables—touched on briefly on p. 22.

Platforms

The first problem is that people use different computers or devices—also known as platforms. There are PCs of various generations (306, 406, 506, Pentiums) and Apple Macintosh in equally different guises. There are also numerous pocket-sized devices. All display differently. So you can put together a page that looks really good on one platform, and it could look very odd on another.

Resolution

The different screen resolutions and colour settings mean that viewers see different amounts of a page. So if you write a 200-word text that fits neatly on a screen 1280 x 1024 at 16-bit colour (a good acceptable standard), someone using the lowest resolution of 640 x 480 at 256 colours will only see 50 words on one screen. Personal organizers or Internet-enabled phones may only display a handful of words. There is not even any guarantee that paragraph spacing will come to your reader as you intended it.

Fonts

Then there are the differences of fonts on the system, and sizes at which users choose to set their email program or browser. Fonts in Netscape always appear much smaller than they do in Explorer. Explorer on a Mac displays the same fonts smaller than on a PC.

Screen resolution choices:

640 x 480
800 x 600
1024 x 768
1152 x 864
1280 x 1024
1600 x 1200
Monitors in pixels

– *available in 256 colours, 16-bit colour, or 32-bit colour*

also

96 x 80
WAP phones

160 x 160
PDA screens

Fonts themselves depend on what individuals have on their own systems, not what you specify on yours. The ones you can rely on that look good on screens—and are universally available—are known as 'web safe' fonts.

Some look good on the screen, Georgia, for example, but don't print out well, and many people require that. Even if you create a print-only version as well as a screen-read version (good practice), it is still better to avoid non-standard fonts. For continuous reading in print, serif fonts (as on this page) are thought to be more readable. On screen, the opposite is true and a font like Verdana gives a clearer, more readable image.

There are two other designed-for-screen fonts, each vying with each other to capture an as yet unsettled market. Microsoft has developed ClearType for its own dedicated Reader software and Adobe has countered with CoolType for *its* dedicated *e*Reader software. They are not available to web designers because they are proprietary fonts.

Old conventions

We should perhaps remember that the book as we know it today took centuries to develop into the brilliant piece of technology it is now.

Space between words did not become standard in western society until the seventh century.

Even after the invention of print in 1455, it took over 50 years to establish conventions such as page numbering, paragraphing, legible typefaces, title pages, chapter divisions, footnotes, indexes, and all the parts that make the book so easy to read and navigate.

We have not yet fully established the conventions that will make the web, and all other electronic environments, as easy to use. And that presents a challenge to those writing for it.

That makes the way you write even more important because you cannot rely on visual aids to help the message.

'Web safe' fonts

Arial
Arial Black
Comic Sans
Courier New
Georgia
Impact
Times New Roman
Tahoma
Trebuchet
Verdana

Parts of a book

cover

title page

publisher info

chapters

footnotes

credits

index

Design and text

Writing for screen display requires an understanding of information design as well as good writing technique. Others may design the look and feel of the site, but the writer needs to be involved in the design process.

For example, the splash page (or welcome page) below occupies a whole screen with white space all round, and contains the following elements:

- a logo;

- a graphic circle with six dynamic menu choices;

- three static choices;

- multilingual options;

- a block of text within the circle that changes according to where the cursor hovers (six different texts).

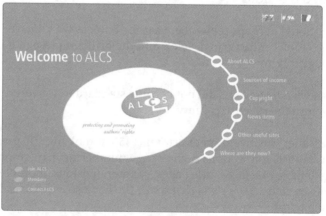

<http://www.alcs.co.uk/>

There is a great deal of functionality on this simple uncluttered page. The constraint for the writer (and also the challenge) is to express the essence of each one of the menu choices in as few words as possible.

An alternative way of doing this is by offering a multi-choice spread, such as this:

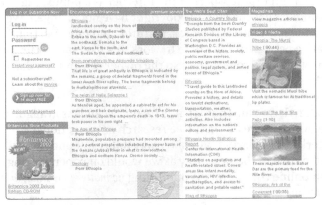

`<http://search.britannica.com/search?query=ethiopia>`

where each choice offers a few words from each article, thus:

Ethiopia
landlocked country of eastern Africa, situated on the Horn of Africa. Ethiopia is bordered on the north by Eritrea, on the east by Djibouti and Somalia, on the south by Kenya, and on the west by The...

See complete article

→ Link to another page

The challenge for the writer here is to make sure the first few words of the article give enough of the flavour of the rest of the piece (which can then be of any length the writer chooses) to indicate whether the rest is of interest.

Design of web pages is as important as the content, but it is not *more* important. Writer and designer will achieve the best results if they work together as a team.

One vital issue to discuss is what the text will look like. As the previous spread explains, typography is hard to control, but you can fight for the best definition. All the research shows that black text on white or off-white screens gives the clearest focus and is best for the reader. Some designers like to put a background pattern behind the text, but this is *always* harder to read. So is a thin sans serif body text (Arial in small sizes) on a rich colour. Even white type on red, black, or blue makes the reader struggle. Make maximum readability a joint priority.

Sharp contrasts of very dark text on very light screens are easiest to read.

Web copyright

'A Book is the Author's Property, 'tis the Child of his Inventions, the Brat of his Brain.'
Daniel Defoe

Another important aspect of the Internet as a publishing medium is that the laws of copyright have not changed. We need the law to protect words, pictures, and music so that creative people can continue to work. It's like, say, protecting a sheep farmer from thieves so the owner continues to have a livelihood.

It's a myth that anything that is freely available is available free. As users, we all want free research or recreational materials, but we also have a responsibility to honour copyright online in the same way as we would on paper. Posting to an online community is publishing *no matter how small that community is.*

Companies generally understand this, but individuals do not always, so it is worth outlining a few salient points.

Remember that there is no redress in British law if you have taken anyone's materials for anything other than personal information. Be aware that

you *may*:

■ copy something from an Internet site for individual use only;

■ print one paper copy from a screen copy;

■ print a list of URLs for websites that you want to circulate.

you *may not*:

■ copy an item you have downloaded for personal use or research again for a friend or colleague;

■ post a copyrighted cartoon, photo, video clip, or anything else on a personal page which is visible to anyone else in an Internet or Intranet community;

■ cut and paste into your own page any material that you didn't write unless it's a very short quotation.

Some people may well feel that copyright isn't appropriate to the Internet, and that if it is hard to protect then no one can enforce it. But enforcement is not the issue. At the moment, and for the time being, copyright is all we've got to protect an individual's work. Copyright is a right whether the work appears on paper, on screen, on film, over radio waves, or just spoken or performed across a room.

So electronic words, music, and pictures are protected by copyright as soon as they are created, and at all stages of being copied onto disks, retrieved from disks, or transmitted from any kind of host computer to any receiving computer.

It's not permissible to post cartoon characters on a personal site, or scan in pictures of football heroes, favourite cars, or technical diagrams, post up tracks of CDs, or block-copy in bits of poems or stories. You can always ask permission from the creators of these things—and most people are happy to negotiate reasonably—but if you don't ask, then actually it is stealing.

Make sure the whole writing team understands this.

See also Part B, pp. 112–114, for more details on legal aspects of publishing.

Hyperlinking has some grey areas of uncertainty. It is almost always acceptable to link to a site's front page.

But links to inside pages or links to a page or image on the linked site that appears to the reader to be part of your page are best not done without permission.

Self-publishing

'A publisher is simply a useful middle-man.'

Oscar Wilde

There are a number of ways of self-publishing on the Internet that fall outside the scope of this book. It is useful, though, for any writer to know what opportunities exist.

Briefly, they include:

- Writing for online magazines—some of which pay (most do not); a good place to start for those who want to see their names in print.

- Book-a-likes (book-sized electronic devices with screens of varying sizes designed for reading continuous texts). The texts displayed on them are e-books, and you can create your own in one of a number of different proprietary formats.

- Any platform using Adobe Portable Document Format (PDF) which is a universal standard for preserving the original appearance—fonts, formatting, colours, and graphics—of any source document, regardless of the application and platform used to create it (see also p. 52).

- Notebook PCs or dedicated tablet hardware using Microsoft Reader format (LIT)—electronic reading software designed for easy screen reading.

- Coding up your own web pages (in HTML or XML)—the coding used by software browsers.

- Making available plain vanilla text (ASCII) or word-processor files.

- Print on Demand—paperbacks supplied by new e-publishers on your behalf from electronic files or scanned from an existing text (the author generally pays for this service and it is very close to vanity publishing).

- Relationships with the new e-publishers who will allow you to self-publish (again at your own expense) in return for providing a showcase for your work on their own sites.

If you are using the Internet as a new medium of creative expression, then you can afford to ignore most of the rules in the rest of this book. Not all of them, however, since good structure, interesting content, and acceptable spelling and grammar still tend to be elements of good web writing.

Nevertheless, you can experiment with the spaces that hypertext offers. Whereas information-based pages essentially present ways of springboarding from one area of a site to another at the user's convenience, creative use of hypertext can alter the whole reading experience.

A few far-sighted artistic people are experimenting and trying to find a new entertainment medium. But no one of genius has yet used hypertext linking so that it becomes an absorbing experience. No Shakespeares have shown others the way.

Entertainment, at whatever artistic level, depends on a team bringing stories or situations to life. Where the Internet scores is that those stories can be visual, musical, and filmic. More than that, they can involve the user in such a way that they feel a part of the story. No other medium has been able to stretch the boundaries between fiction and real life in the way the Internet can.

The Internet is, after all, a delivery mechanism and of course it can deliver entertainment. Perhaps you—the reader of this book—will be the first to succeed dramatically.

Meanwhile, the rest of us will stick with informational web writing.

Some creative writing sites to look at	
literary hypertext	<http://www.eastgate.com/> <http://www.hypertextkitchen.com/>
poetry	<http://www.poetsoflondon.com/>
words as art	<http://coda.drexel.edu/wordplay/>
journalism	<http://www.thevines.com/>

Linearity

*'Begin at the beginning,'
the King said,
gravely, 'and go
on till you come
to the end:
then stop'*

Lewis Carroll, *Alice in Wonderland*

Informational writing is often linear. That is to say, it has a chronological flow or logical sequence. The writer takes readers through a stage-by-stage argument.

But the web is, by its very nature, multidirectional. Users arrive at a particular page in a number of ways. The page might branch off a link on the front page of the site, or it might be linked from a totally different site. This means the step-by-step approach does not work well. Users expect to click backwards and forwards, to the top of the page and to parts within it. The user controls the appearance of the screen as well as the order in which to read from it.

The web writer can, all the same, create a linear narrative by forcing the reader to get to the end of a section of text (also known as an 'information chunk') before clicking on to the next. This technique, successfully used in PowerPoint presentations, relies on having a single forward click at the end of each piece.

Back to   Back one   next page   skip to end
Beginning   page

The web displays things we've so far had on paper, film, or airwaves. And we haven't quite outgrown the expectations we bring with us from those forms. All are generally in a linear construction.

We even use linear terminology to talk about the web. Even the notion of a 'page' is a linear one. They are not pages at all; they're files.

Interactivity

A web author needs to decide when to keep the visitors concentrating on the mainline track and when the message is secure enough to let them go off on a branch line. Too many branches result in the mental equivalent of a crash. Too few, and you're not really using the power of hypertext.

Hypertext was originally conceived as a 'text space', but something rather better than text. It is named by analogy with the well-defined mathematical concept of 'hyperspace', i.e. space with more than three dimensions. The 'hyper' in 'hypertext' means 'above'. Hypertext offers one opening (the front page) and many outcomes (all the other pages).

Each page is a hypertext unit; one links to another. The user chooses in which order to read, and that is what makes the web interactive. Even though the person constructing the page, or suite of pages, may have a sensible order in mind, that may not be the pattern the user observes.

The same is true of this book, which has an internal logical order but can be read spread by spread. The difference is that you can flick through the book and get a sense of where you are in it and what went before. On the web, you only see the page you are looking at, so the writer will always have to decide when to repeat information and when to assume the viewer can go somewhere else for it.

The person who designs the structure of the site will decide how the text is chopped up to fit into the overall design and what navigational aids to use to lead from one part of the site to the other. If you are not that person, but are fitting into a team, you may find this very constraining. It is helpful to talk about the usefulness of the interactivity on the site in question.

end two

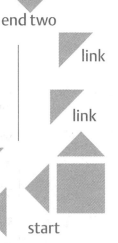

link

link

dead
end

link

end one

link

link

link

start

3 Considering purpose

There are many choices to make before the planning and the writing begins. A clear sense of purpose is an absolute necessity before you begin to build the site. This chapter looks at reasons for having a website, what to put on it, and what your audience demands.

Goals

First, do you really need a full-blown website or just a single-page presence? It is not necessary to have one just because everyone else has jumped on the bandwagon. It may be fun to put together at first, but constant maintenance is expensive in time and resources. And the Internet is fashion-conscious, so even a website with static materials can show its age within a couple of years and may need redesigning.

It's best if everyone involved takes a long-term perspective. Otherwise it may be like many other new ventures – initial enthusiasm which then peters out.

In order to clarify your thoughts, see how you might 'sell' the idea of a website either to yourself or to your boss. What would make it a success? For example, which of these goals could a web presence accomplish over the next year?

- enable you to be found by anyone anywhere;

- enhance your image;

- save postage costs;

- reduce staff time in answering repetitive queries;

- help with processing member information;

- keep in touch with what members or clients want;

- carry content that would replace a newsletter;

- replace or reduce the need for other publications (information pamphlets, catalogues, and brochures);

- keep the association or customers up to the minute with daily, weekly, monthly or annual developments;

- circulate information out of pure altruism;

- display and describe products or services or creative work;

- make significant savings through sales direct from the site.

If you haven't ticked at least three of the boxes, think carefully. Image and visibility may be appealing, but if there are no other benefits, then is that enough of a 'sell'? Circulating information for its own sake is a worthy aim for someone with the time to do it, but if a company does that (and some do) then there should be another benefit resulting from it.

Visitor benefits

It is likely that if several of the goals above are achievable, site visitors will benefit too. So look at the measures of success listed again and consider them all from the point of view of your intended visitors. Is it an advantage to them if you can be found easily or if you save money on postage. What do *they* gain?

Think about downsides. Perhaps users get what they need immediately and without hassle, but is it going to cost them more in paper and ink to print out your promotion materials, and would they rather wait a day to get it in the post?

All these are important and essential considerations, and you cannot begin to think about the site in detail until you are clear about the gains and benefits. A good starting place is to look at other sites.

Evaluating other websites

The standard advice to any budding writer is to read a lot and to absorb what others have done in the same genre. It is the same with websites. If you want to write well for the web, look at sites like the one you are going to create. What do you like about them and what does not work for you?

Make a list of features you want to emulate and note those you do not—bearing in mind the intended gains already identified.

The chances are that a successful site will instantly answer the 'who-what-when-where' query quartet (these journalistic coat-hangers turn up again in Chapter 5).

Who

Everyone wants to know who is speaking, so look for:

■ author and publisher details (individual or corporate);

■ mention of any quality checks or referencing of the information;

■ an email link on every page so visitors can always see 'who's talking' because this gives credibility to what is being said.

And do they know who *you* are? A good site should be able to address different types of people who all come to the site for a variety of reasons. So if it makes assumptions that are irksome or seem to patronize visitors, think about how that feels and how you might address them differently.

Look for page counters that say you are the x thousandth visitor since 1 January. The chances are you are not, and it is a giveaway that the site creators are anxious about visitor numbers and are trying to create a buzz that does not reflect reality. You'd be right to be suspicious of that and you'd be right to avoid doing it yourself.

What

Give a clear title and first sentence so the visitor can see instantly what is likely to be on the page. This has a double function, as the title and first few words are what will show onscreen when a search engine presents results, so it should clearly:

■ state the aims and objectives of the site on the front page;

■ describe each individual page.

The page title also helps users remember why they book-marked a particular page.

When

One of the first things people want to know is how current the page is—is it this year's Edinburgh Festival programme or last year's? Are they reading recent pharmaceutical research or has it lost currency? So you'll be looking for:

■ creation and modification dates;

■ clearly marked archival information.

Age may or may not matter. Stamping a revision date on every page may not be necessary for all types of site and can sometimes look a little sorry as the months pass. Just copyright symbol and year may be enough.

Where

It is useful to know in what country the site originated in case 'they do things differently there'. A corporate affiliation can be enough, but even then it's helpful to know if one is visiting XCompany UK or XCompany USA. Look for:

■ where in the world the site is;

■ details of the origin of any data or information.

These points will vary according to the project. But once you are clear in your mind what works for you on other sites, you will be closer to deciding how to construct your own.

| # Content

Having anchored the 'who-what-when-where' features, move on to the content itself. If you review other sites, it may help to crystallize what you want to achieve. After all, critical evaluation is a backdrop against which you will later be testing your own site.

■ Does the resource appear to be honest and genuine?

■ Is it the result of a personal hobby-horse? And if it is, then is that charmingly eccentric or potentially pernicious, if not illegal?

■ Is the resource available in another format (e.g. a book or CD-ROM) and would it be preferable in that format?

■ Could any of the materials infringe copyright? This is hard to judge with text, but the quality of the graphics may offer some clues.

■ Is the information well researched? If it is, then it will quote sources.

■ Is any bias made clear and of an acceptable level?

One of the difficulties in looking critically at content on the Internet is that it all looks rather the same. Obviously, there is good design and bad design, but on the whole there are only three or four typefaces that actually work on screens, so the basic text has a look of uniformity about it. It's generally in one of the fonts that everyone can rely on all browsers to have (see pp. 26–7).

There are few external clues, as there are in the print world—feel and thickness of the paper, feel of the print, quality of the spine—which tell the reader something about the value the originators have invested in the text. Physical properties act as hidden persuaders and we *are* influenced by them.

This means the reader has to be constantly vigilant and judgemental. Everything is out there: the gems in amongst the slush.

Informal content

Posting content online is, in effect, publication, even when it only goes before a limited community. A password-protected site may have one set of rules; a company intranet another; a school displaying children's work yet another.

Ground rules are important to ensure that whatever is posted in a public place reflects the site's ethos. Here are a few of the issues you may want to consider both on other sites and when thinking about your own.

■ Decide whether more informal parts of a limited community, such as chat rooms, conferences, or forums, should have more relaxed rules about accuracy than the high standards and refining that published work aspires to.

■ Libel can damage people's reputations. Even in a closed community, laws of libel and privacy apply.

■ Think about prejudice (such as racism, gender, fascism, or religion). Make sure nothing is abusive on the site.

■ Agree on how to moderate private areas so no one can post messages or display material that is inappropriate or disturbing to other readers.

All these—and many similar—issues show the need for exceptional vigilance on the part of the writer-editor.

Audience

Of course, it comes down (as it always does) to whom you are addressing. The Introduction talked about the changing role of the writer. The 'audience' has changed too. On the printed page, it is the 'reader'; when the words are on a computer screen, they go to an 'end-user'. The difference is one of tone. 'End-use' is 'the final specific use to which a product is put'. The user is rapacious and wants the material for a purpose; the reader is someone to woo with a leisurely unfolding of an argument.

In the last century, novelist or essayist alike thought carefully about the level at which to address the reader. It would flatter to regard the reader as a choice spirit, quick on the uptake, who would not need every allusion stressed or every point hammered home. To signpost every reference with inverted commas, and—God forbid—to translate from the Latin or the French, would be to insult the reader.

Never assume the reader wants to read what you have written.

On the web, users no longer read a text (as in 'study, familiarize'), but scan it looking only for what is useful to them. Rapid-reading tutors have always taught politicians and businessmen to skim-read diagonally across the page; on the Internet, people scroll in screenful-sized chunks.

So make it easy for them to do that. Structure the site, and its tone of voice, for the people whose needs and expectations you hope to satisfy. They might be a diverse bunch of experts and novices in the field. Writing to appeal to all of them is not easy. You can't afford to talk down, and they'll leave the site in droves if you make the writing too dense.

To make sure you are attracting all skills levels in your users, ask yourself:

■ What is your site for?

■ Who does it aim to attract?

■ How should you address your audience?

Here are some sample answers to these questions: different projects will answer them in other ways.

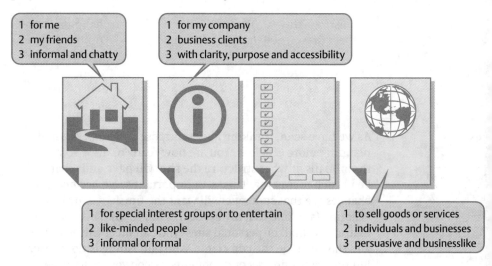

1 for me
2 my friends
3 informal and chatty

1 for my company
2 business clients
3 with clarity, purpose and accessibility

1 for special interest groups or to entertain
2 like-minded people
3 informal or formal

1 to sell goods or services
2 individuals and businesses
3 persuasive and businesslike

Profile

Do you have (or need) an audience profile? If it is for a family, local community or club, or worldwide special interest group, then no, probably not. But if it is to advertise products and services, then profiling helps fine-tune the target market. It is easier then for the writers to reach that audience.

They need to know:

■ why they are writing content for a particular page;

■ what the reader needs to know;

■ how one page relates to others in the web;

■ what standard conventions there are for a type of site;

■ assumptions people in different parts of the world may make.

Online questionnaires help develop a visitor profile. An incentive, or gift, often tempts visitors to fill these in.

Think worldwide: how wise was it to call a car 'Nova' when 'no va' in Spanish means 'it doesn't go'.

4 | Planning

As we have seen, thinking about purpose and audience make planning more efficient. You are now ready to draw some thumbnails of what structure the site will have and what will be in each main area. This is an important stage because the chances are that someone will want the finished copy by a deadline (and one that always seems too soon). This does not matter on small or personal sites: you can meet the deadline and then change the copy later. Web publishing is not static. But on a large site, second thoughts can be very expensive because of all the changes they require. So think first.

Process

How much time (as a percentage of the whole) would you expect to spend on each of these essential processes? Use the diagram below as a basis for jotting down your first thoughts—not what you think you *should* do, but how you like to work. It may be personally instructive to look back later and check against the reality of what happened on a particular project.

| Brainstorming with others | + | planning | + | drafting | + | editing | = | total 100% |

In a company, the planning stage is the most vital. It's important for an individual as well, but if you are working in a team, you need to be sure everyone has agreed the plan before starting to write. Plan the site in detail drawing on the brainstorming session. Then circulate the plan and get everyone's approval in *writing*.

Navigation

As the writer, it may or may not be your job to plan the navigation structure. Sometimes the team specifies the central elements and the designer comes up with a concept and structure.

The theory is that no one should ever be more than three clicks away from the information they want. It's a useful goal, but not always possible to put into practice. You can do your very best to anticipate what your users need; sometimes you'll succeed.

The difficulty is that web writing is not static. If your visitor makes Choice A here, what are the ramifications for Choice B there? It is rarely obvious. You can take a linear or a spider approach. Or store writing chunks in a database for retrieval in any order.

The three clicks theory:
It should not take more than three mouse clicks for visitors to find what they are looking for.

Linear

A linear site usually looks like this (though it can take a number of forms):

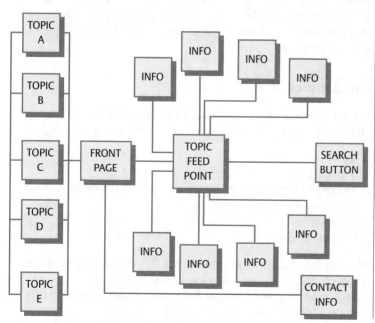

Spider

A spider or 'mind-map' site looks like this (the idea being that anything can link to anything else and the user does not need a sense of where they are in the site).

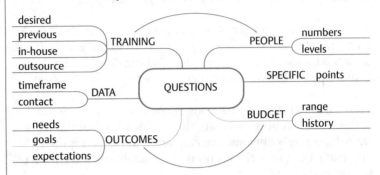

Dynamic site

Dynamically generated pages are pulled into a template as the user requests the page—search engines, for example, work in this way. You type in a search word and the engine goes and looks for the matching results. Membership organizations that ask for registration details before allowing entry are frequently dynamic too. They present pages to each member with personalized elements.

Site statistics

1000 'hits' does not mean 1000 people have visited a page.

A pageview is a single downloaded page. A 'hit' is everything that is on a pageview. Each element counts as one hit, e.g.

A logo or picture	1 hit
The main text	1 hit
Six graphics buttons that change colour when the mouse rolls over them	12–18 hits
An animation	4 hits
A banner advertisement	12 hits

The last two can be any number, but this example has a minimum of 30 hits on the pageview because 30 items are downloaded. So when people tell you their site gets 1000 hits a day, do a bit of division to get a realistic picture.

Top levels

Any planning decisions involve deciding how to handle the following.

> **Welcome (or Home or Splash) page:** a concise introductory page that indicates the site's purpose and then presents a logical branch of choices: 6–8 is generally plenty, though large information sites need more.
>
> **Main menu topics:** It is useful to have those top-level choices as a mini table of contents at the top or left-hand side of every page.
>
> **Sub-topics:** These can branch out from the main topics and may be displayed as sub-menus in a variety of ways.

Whatever the underlying structure, the editorial team has to make decisions that the design and technical team will implement, such as:

- whether to include a sitemap (this can be a sign of weakness as the site should be intuitive without the need for a map, but it depends on the complexity and size of the whole);

- whether it is clearer or more confusing to split one topic into two (and conversely, whether to combine several headings);

- whether sub-topic X really is best branching off main topic A or whether it should be somewhere else;

- whether to duplicate information in various parts of the site or have alternative, context-related choices leading to the same information.

It is useful if the person who is going to be responsible for writing the copy is involved in discussions on navigation. It will not matter so much on a large site for which different templates have been set up to help individual writers, but even then, the writing benefits from drawing on an overall view of where any particular page fits into the navigational structure of the whole.

| # Page width

Look at the page below. You can just make out the first two lines of the piece running from the extreme left to the extreme right of the screen with 20 words in the line (on a browser set at 1280 x 1024 16-bit colour and full screen).

The scroll bar (right) shows that visible text is about 25 per cent of the whole article

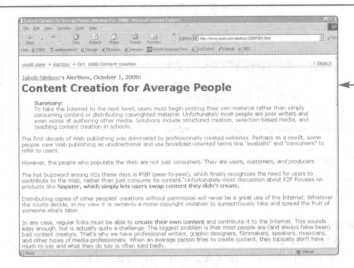

Jakob Nielsen's Alertbox <http://www.useit.com/alert-box/20001001.html>

It reads:

'The first decade of web publishing was dominated by professionally created websites. Perhaps as a result, some people view Web publishing as unidirectional and use broadcast-oriented terms like "eyeballs" and "consumers" to refer to users.'

At nine words to a line, this is comfortable to read. But it is not possible to fix a line length like this on a screen. Monitor resolutions vary (as we saw on p. 26) and not everybody has the screen maximized to the full window all the time. Jakob Nielsen (whose Alertbox on web usability is worth reading) knows this and makes no attempt to design for page width.

An alternative approach is this one, where the designer has put the main text in a table to force a comfortable reading width (the same browser setting as the one on the previous page leaves half the screen empty):

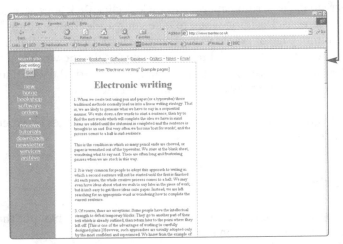

<http://www.mantex.co.uk/>

The scroll bar shows that visible text is about 10 per cent of the whole article.

The secret to fixing page width is to put body text into an invisible table. So ask your designers to fix the table at a maximum of 10–12 words to a line. At present screen resolutions, this is a good reading line length. A greater length often results in readers losing their way.

One advantage of fixing a reading width is that the rest of the screen is still there, so a panel on the right or the left can give navigational details. Every page needs a sense of location, otherwise those who are parachuted in from another site are lost before they hit the ground.

Remember that sometimes your users will just have a page reference taking them straight in. Make sure they do not land in an anonymous maze with no way out except the browser's back button.

Tip:
To fix a line width of 10–12 words, you need to set the table width at between 500 and 650, e.g.

```
<table
border="0"
cellpadding="10"
cellspacing="10"
width="500">
 <tr>
  <td>Body
text</td>
 </tr>
</table>
```

| # Page length

It is curious that we call a computer 'file' a 'page'. It is probably because the print metaphor is so familiar.

Papyrus scrolls were often more than 60 feet (18 metres) long.

Screen pages scroll; paper pages flick. A click-flick goes across two screens. Deciding when to take your reader down a long scrolling page or across to another one is far from easy. It is irritating for the reader if you, as the writer, make the wrong decision. Knowing your audience helps. It is critical to consider how much time they expect to spend on the page.

You have two choices: cut everything into short pages or expect readers to scroll.

Scrolling

Navigate long pages sparingly with up buttons

Back to the top

If the answer to the three questions below is 'yes', then put the complete document on one continuous web page.

■ Will they read all of it?

■ Will they use the document for reference?

■ Will they print it out?

The upside is that it uses less telephone time (a serious consideration where people are paying by connection time). It is better for documents written for print. And more user-friendly for bookmarking or quoting as reference.

The downside is that viewers will not see what is further down the page unless they are sufficiently interested to scroll. You can use clickable subheadings and summaries at the top to give the gist.

Chunking

If the answer to the next trio is 'yes', then divide your pages up into small, digestible chunks. Between 200 and 400 words is plenty.

- Do they want to be amused?

- Do they want quick information?

- Will they read different parts at different times?

The upside is that all the text should be visible on a single screen at high screen resolutions, which makes it easier for people to get a sense of what is on the page.

The downside is that users may get irritated if they have to step through several pages, even where they are choosing to read a longer document non-sequentially.

Pages emerged in Europe in the second century AD.

The third way

The compromise is to do both. Cut an essay or paper into chunks for readers who are happy to read on screen with a one-phrase blurb indicating what's in each chunk in the hyperlink area. On another button, offer a

Printer-friendly version of this story

This can be in a continuous HTML document or plain ASCII. If you do this, remember to include an attribution on the printer-friendly version so readers know where it came from, such as:

This article was printed from
<name of website> + page reference and date
Copyright ©200x
[All rights reserved]

Consider also whether to make longer documents into .PDF files for downloading into the Acrobat Reader (see overleaf).

The upside is that pages can be designed for print.

The downside is that not everyone has—or wants to go and get—the free Reader software. Also, pages with graphics features may be large files and take a long time to download.

Long documents

Of course, there will be occasions when you want to write 'normally' and assume your audience will print out and read from paper.

When you offer documents in an archive, try to give the file size, number of pages and date of the document. It will help readers decide if they want to download them.

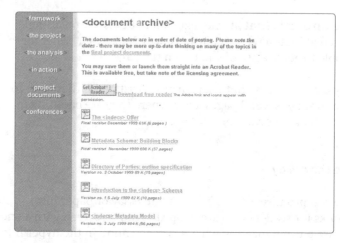

<http://www.indecs.org/>

Print

As we saw on the previous page, printing out a long web page is not always satisfactory.

A rule of thumb is that two 640 x 480 screens-worth of information will print out on one sheet of A4. Even that is making assumptions about screens and printers that one cannot make. But it is irritating for the user to find that the last printed page carries no more than the URL and page title.

The best way of displaying discursive work on the Internet is in Acrobat Reader as a .PDF file. This stands for Portable Document Format and is based on page–description–language technology. It can be properly designed and displayed, like any published document.

In theory, files can be shared, viewed, navigated, and printed exactly as intended by anyone with a free Adobe Acrobat Reader, though there can be a slight problem because of the different standard paper sizes used in the UK and the US. It depends whether the publication is in portrait or landscape, but either way, if it's laid out for the slightly larger size then one or two lines might spill over onto another page.

It's best to design your document to fit within the width of A4 (210 mm) and the height of US Letter (279 mm). So make a custom page size for your document of 210 mm wide x 279 mm deep.

The trouble here is that the software expects standard sizes, so when it distils your document to make a .PDF file, the file will open in Acrobat set to A4 or US Letter size. The solution here is to crop all of the pages down to 210 x 279 mm, and resave the file.

Tip:
Let your users know that they can get the free Acrobat Reader at `<http://www.adobe.com/prodindex/acrobat/>`

Word documents may not always convert identically to a .PDF file with line-for-line accuracy. This is because Word's printing technology has a weakness in this area—but this may be fixed in later versions. A dedicated desktop publishing package tends to do a better job.

Security

A second reason for converting to .PDF is that it protects you against plagiarism. You are likely to feel more of a sense of ownership over discursive—perhaps even literary—work than you do about the functional prose we are concerned with in most of this book.

Acrobat protects your document to some extent because it cannot be edited, as a Word document can. It is now possible to save .PDF files with a number of different levels of security. So, for example, the user could have permission to print the file, but would be unable to block-copy any part of it. It is possible too, to set an expiry date after which the user would not be able to open the file. All this is very useful for web-published material, but as with all encryption it's easy enough to find software that unlocks security mechanisms.

| # Collaborative writing

As the chart in the Introduction (p. 11) shows, writing and planning frequently involves people collaborating on a project. Perhaps a writing team is involved in a large website and needs to share work. Or perhaps co-authors are simply using the convenience of the Internet as a medium for the exchange of ideas.

Part of the planning stage is to decide amongst the team on joint strategies. It can save hours, if not days, of frustration.

When the work is electronic, it is hard to see what a colleague has done to alter it. In the days of paper, anyone could respond to scribbled margin notes and ignore them if they didn't agree. Now everyone will need to invent their own codes of practice because the paper paradigms do not apply. It is tedious to read two versions of an electronic file line for line against one another. Here are a few ideas:

General

- Decide at the beginning what software you will use and agree on how people in a group will handle revisions.

- Decide every time the file changes hands who has the 'live master' copy and try to ensure that only one person is working on the current master version at any given time.

- If it is a large project with several 'live' files, make sure one person coordinates them all before the presentation version is ready for assessment.

- Agree on a House Style (see pp. 84–85 and 110–11). This might involve talking about capitalization style, punctuation, grammar and spelling, references, and sense.

Tip:
Agree beforehand on how to edit HTML files. Do not edit them in Word as it adds code that programmers will have to strip out.

HTML files

Use the Comment command and stipulate that everyone should precede the comment with their own initial, like this:

```
<!– "JD: comment" –>
```

■ In a graphical HTML editor, the comment will show in coloured text on screen, but not once it is in the browser. In non-graphical programs, other writers should be alert to the possibility of comments from colleagues.

Emails

■ Contain comments or edited text within personal delimiters such as ### or [ ] or << >> so the next person can search for changes.

■ If you are collaborating by email, it's usually helpful to return the original and interrupt it with a double carriage return every time you suggest a change—so it is easy to see.

Word files

Either:

■ Agree on and use different screen text colours or highlighter markings for each person who is working on a multi-authored file. This shows each member of the team who has said what.

■ Co-writers could write comments and queries using the annotations function (Insert Menu / Comment).

Or:

■ Use the footnote function as an insertion point for a comment (Insert Menu / Footnote)—this is better for printouts.

■ Use Word's Track Changes facility (Tools Menu) to view changes between versions.

If taking emailed text into a word-processor, remember to remove hard carriage returns.

Remember to keep the previous versions. This can be an informative way to reflect on the development of the task. It also gives evidence of the work that has been done.

Tip:
In Microsoft Word, go to Format / Autoformat, scroll down the option box, and select Email. This will remove all the hard returns in an email.

5 | Good web writing

So far we have looked at the general importance of deciding who you are writing for, and how to plan the general structure accordingly. This chapter reviews the writing itself. The next chapter looks at revising your work for screen display.

In a book like this one, the design and layout are integral to the writing because each topic occupies a two-page spread with graphic elements amplifying the main points. It's obvious at a glance what's on the page.

In the electronic environment, viewers rarely see a whole page and different browsers display different proportions of it, differently, as explained on p. 26. It is impossible to control visual appearance, and this means that signposting has to help the reader absorb the message.

We are used to signposting in newspapers, where cross-heads, captions, and pictures catch the eye and lead people into the whole story. These are hidden persuaders, seducing the reader into looking at one story rather than another. Every piece of writing takes account of such 'tricks of the trade'. You can ignore them—and why not; freshness and verve come from breaking the rules. But a rule rejected because of its constraints feeds originality; a rule rejected through lack of experience results in poor writing.

'No rule is so general, which admits not some exception.'

Robert Burton: *Anatomy of Melancholy*

Let's call them conventions rather than rules and consider:

- how to construct a news story;
- what makes a punchy heading;
- why plain prose is better than gobbledegook;
- how to read your own work critically.

Principles

None of us really knows what good web writing is. You have to test out a technology to see what it can deliver, and the web is still at the 'flicker' stage; films used to be called 'the flicks' when the industry was in its infancy.

All the same, a number of people have seen trends, and though they may prove to be wrong, what follows is based on personal experience and observation as well as current thinking. The following trends are developed in this and the next chapter and there is a checklist in Part B, p. 105:

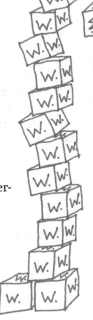

- White space helps web display so write in 'chunks'— 30-word paragraphs separated by a line space work well. But vary paragraph lengths. This is so that the eye can easily take in the point and can orientate on a scrolling page.

- Readers want to grasp the main point at the top of the screen; it saves time. They'll move away if nothing grabs their attention.

- Heading and hyperlink wording can be easily misunderstood. Moderate user-testing can help you get both of them unambiguous.

- Random linking of chunks to other chunks will not satisfy visitors in the long term—only while they are surfing round to get the feel of your site. Organize material in a logical order even though you know your users will not necessarily read it in that order.

One of the problems facing web writers is that everyone thinks they can write, because everyone *does* write. Not everyone writes well. First-generation websites allowed a great deal of unedited writing, sometimes even making a virtue out of zaniness and 'attitude'. But the web is maturing, and while 'attitude' can sometimes be refreshing, it can also be offputting.

Your job may also include convincing managers within organizations that you can write and that you understand web style.

Word-processing

Tip:
Always check for spelling errors using your word-processing software, but never rely on it.

If you are comfortable composing straight onto a word-processor, stick to that for writing content for the web. There is no need to start in a graphical web-page creation package (such as FrontPage, PageMill, Site Aid, or Dreamweaver). If you are distracted by an unfamiliar technology, you will not be able to concentrate on the writing itself.

If you are totally consistent in the way in which you word-process, then it will be far easier to transfer from one program to another. Search and replace techniques for the coding will come into play when the text is finalized.

Web-creation tools can convert

```
<Heading 1> or
<A Head> etc.

into  HTML code

<H1></H1>
<H2></H2> etc.
```

Select the word-processor's <Heading 1> for your main page title, <Heading 2> for sub-headings – and so on. The headings may become graphics buttons. Different colours can help to identify main or sub-directory topics. Always use Normal for the body text for every section. Ideally your web designer will use Cascading Style Sheets and Normal will transpose into whatever the designer chooses for text on the entire site. It doesn't matter what fonts you use—whatever is comfortable to your eye. Times New Roman at 12 pt is a good standard because it shows up well on all screens.

Good word-processing practice

If the technology gets in the way of writing, then ignore what follows. If not, it will help in the transfer to the coded page if you:

- Use only one space after a full stop. Using two or three spaces is an old typist's technique and is not web-friendly. More space makes the sentences float apart, making life difficult for the reader.

- Indicate hyperlinks in an obvious way so that the person doing the coding knows what you want. For example:

  Join our e-mentoring service <— JD PLEASE LINK TO THE QUESTIONNAIRE SURVEY —>

- Do not hyphenate end-of-line word breaks because they may be in the middle of the line on someone else's screen.

- Use a proper dash, not a single hyphen, when you want to make an aside: it is the correct punctuation and shows up better on screen.

- Use 'smart quotes' (as here, rather than the prime mark ' because the curve carries the eye forward). Single inverted commas are UK style; double ones are favoured in the US.

- Insert symbols and foreign characters.

Non-standard characters, and dashes and quotation marks, are tricky to code in HTML because whatever you do, you cannot guarantee that all browsers will display them in the same way. But it sometimes works if you cut and paste from the word-processed document into a graphical HTML program. (The codes for these are given on p. 83.)

- Do not use bullets or asterisks in lists—define a style called 'Bulleted lists' instead. The reason for this is that bullets often transfer unreliably in HTML programs and someone might have to take out each one individually and then redefine the style of the section.

- Avoid using tables unless you have tested how they transfer.

- Look for rogue, hidden line-breaks at the ends of lines, especially where emailed text has been pasted in.

- Some writers use double carriage returns for new paragraphs. Check what happens in the HTML program. If it adds more white space between paragraphs than expected, you may have to search and replace using one carriage return instead, and define the paragraph style in your word-processor so that it adds a gap after each paragraph.

These points do not apply in all circumstances, but anyone transferring from Microsoft Word to FrontPage or Dreamweaver will find it saves time to observe them at word-processing stage rather than later. Do a test run on sample material to see what happens when you cut and paste between programs.

There are two dash marks, the en dash
–
Ctrl+Num+ -

and the em dash
—
Alt+Ctrl+Num+ -

'' = smart quotes

(in Word, go to Tools/AutoCorrect/ AutoFormat As You Type and tick the box to replace 'straight quotes' with 'smart quotes'

' = a prime mark

Tip:
Print the text double-spaced and read it on paper. Try setting it in an unfamiliar font—you'll notice new errors.

In word-processing

 Don't!

ever edit an HTML document in Word (it adds its own code).

| # First draft

Once you have a plan for the site (or the part of the site you are responsible for), spend some time identifying what will go in each sub-topic, and that means a single page or a suite of pages related to one topic. Background materials may come from printed sources or from conversations with colleagues or from your own personal life or work.

Starting from print

Although it is a bad idea to cut and paste brochure material straight into the planned-out sections, the probability is that you will be starting from some pre-written materials. After all, your organization has already done some thinking and there's no need to throw it all away. It's quite useful to go through a paper copy with a highlighter and mark up what you absolutely *must* repeat word for word. Be very exacting in what you let through; a list of benefits, perhaps, or membership services. Lists of sponsors must obviously go in, but you can tuck them away in an interior part of the site even if they are prominent in the brochure.

When you have blocked out the sections that will transfer to the web verbatim, assign them to a location on the web plan.

Avoid jargon—
these were
generated by
<http://www.
dack.com/web/
bullshit.html>

visualize next-
generation markets

reinvent 24/365
e-markets

target innovative
e-services

Then read everything else very carefully. Extract the sense from it and see if you can rewrite each page in short, cogent chunks. People tend to skim-read on the web, so they need key concepts.

What can you shorten? Try reducing a 25-word mission statement to a 3-word strap line, as in:

The listening bank

If the managing director wants the full mission statement onsite, you can click-link it to your strap line.

Outlining

Some people need to map out what they want to say in diagrammatic form first; others think as they write. There is no correct way, though for most people a useful strategy is:

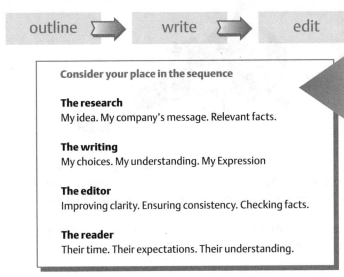

outline ➤ write ➤ edit ➤ feedback

Consider your place in the sequence

The research
My idea. My company's message. Relevant facts.

The writing
My choices. My understanding. My Expression

The editor
Improving clarity. Ensuring consistency. Checking facts.

The reader
Their time. Their expectations. Their understanding.

It is easier to concentrate on the topic rather than on the way you are writing. The only thing to be aware of is that it can be hard to be self-critical once you've written something down. It really depends on personality: some people like revising and others try to get it right first time. You could say 'getting it right' is like bricklaying: building slowly and not adding a new row until the foundation is solid enough to hold up the house. There are different ways of doing that. What's important is to have an overview of the architecture of the whole house.

You can do this on paper or with a word-processor. Microsoft Word users may find it useful to work in Document Map or Outline mode as it helps with keeping the full structure in mind. It is also easier to move whole sections to a different place. You *will* want to do this. Several times. It isn't a weakness to change your mind about what goes where as you begin to write.

Remember, if the overall plan is a team effort, to log the reasons for any changes so you can justify them later.

The tadpole structure

News stories very often follow a tadpole structure. The 'meat' is all in the head and the extra bits in the tail.

Most readers will only see the introduction. Make sure everything important is in it.

This is a useful pattern for a web page because users only scroll down a page if they really want to know more. So give the main points at the top of the page, and let details unfold lower down.

It is often helpful to give your reader links to the other details at the top of the page so they can click down to the paragraph they want.

A party game

This sort of writing has a step-by-step underpinning. It's quite instructive, in a group, to do it as a game of Consequences; fold down your piece of paper at each 'step' so the next person you pass it to cannot read what you have written.

- *Step 1.* **Who, What, Where**
  Write a paragraph of not more than 25 words saying what the event is.
  —Tom met Mary at 4.30 in the park and now they are getting married.

- *Step 2.* **Why**
  Write a brief explanation containing essential facts about the event.
  —Tom liked parks and was studying floral arrangements.

Step 3. **Because**
Give some background facts to put the story in context.
—They met because they wanted to go for a walk. He said…
she said… And then they…

Step 4. **And** (what the world said)
Support the story with some quotes for and against
—Tom's mum said 'I hope they'll be happy', but his dad
thought they should not see each other for a year.

Step 5. **So** (the consequence was)
Any additional aspect
—Meeting people in parks might be hazardous.

*'Who the Hell
ever reads
the second
paragraph?'*

Hecht and MacArthur in *The
Front Page*

This structure is the standard order for many human-interest
stories and it works well on the web too. The difference is
that you can offer click-links, so people may read sections in
any order.

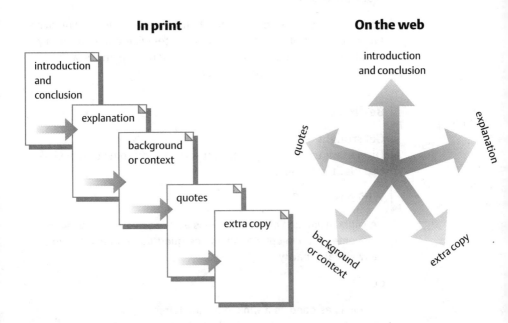

In print

introduction
and
conclusion

explanation

background
or context

quotes

extra copy

On the web

introduction
and conclusion

quotes

explanation

background
or context

extra copy

Although this technique is useful, do not become a slave to it.
Vary it according to your material. Formula writing is dull.
What would a forest be like if all the birdsong were the same?

Summaries

A writer's skill in writing quick-flash summaries is paramount. You have just a handful of words to let readers know the scope and type of information that is lower down the page, or on another one.

The summary can either:

- whet the appetite so they dig deeper into your site to find the details;

or

- provide enough information so they do not have to read any more.

The second is the essence of good web style. It is more flexible and more practical than print style. Though the aim is still the same: to make the reader's task easy even if this means extra work for you.

Print is really the wrong model. Think of other media. The overall word count of a 20-minute radio or television documentary is about a third of 20 minutes of reading from print. A web summary should be even shorter.

Be direct

'*Had I had longer, it would have been shorter*'.

Winston Churchill

Get straight to the point.
Direct language works better on screen than marketing-speak.
Use plain language.

Which is better?

A slight inclination of the cranium is as adequate as a spasmodic movement of one optic of an equine quadruped utterly devoid of any visual capacity.

or

A nod is as good as a wink to a blind horse.

or just

It's all the same.

The eyes don't read; they move across a line of print in a series of jerks and pauses. During the pauses the eyes take a 'photograph'. When the eyes come to a full stop, the brain organizes the photographs so that the message makes sense. If the brain comes across something it doesn't understand, it will instruct the eyes to 're-photograph'. If this happens a lot, the reader will give up and move on to something else. So you have to consider the complexity and length of your sentences, as well as the meaning of your words, as you write.

Techniques you can use to be concise include:

- lists;

- short phrases, not full sentences;

- brief statements.

A list like this is easy to take in at a glance, but balance that against the number of lines it is going to take up on the screen. Every line near the top of a web page must earn its shelf space. Make sure that you are not providing too little information in the effort to be concise.

Look at sign writing—brevity at its extreme. The aim here is to convey information quickly, and it doesn't much matter if you cut short the grammar. What you don't want is a sign that is ambiguous or misleading. Here are some favourites

> Beware cross traffic
> Same day cleaners – 48 hour service
> Worn tyres kill – buy here

and just in case you secretly don't think care with words is important, one single wrong letter can change a meaning:

> Slow—concealed entrances
> No overtaking for the next 200 yrs

What you are trying to do is to give information and to make the reader's task as easy as possible. Hard writing makes easy reading.

'Readers are invariably in a hurry to get to the point. They want to ride down a motorway, not thrash about in the Hampton Court Maze.'

The Plain English Campaign

Hard writing makes easy reading

| # Menu choices

Take a great deal of care over your choice of menu words—headings (text or graphics buttons) that lead to documents or other subheadings on the same or another page. Do they clearly indicate what the user will find by following that choice? Can they be misunderstood? Have you checked that you use the same phrase each time to lead to a page? (If not, your reader will think there is something new and be frustrated if it leads to a page they have already seen.) Are you using company jargon that won't be meaningful outside?

Finding just the right names for menu items is of prime importance, and it will pay off to spend a lot of time thinking up:

- synonyms and other ways of expressing the same concept;

- ways in which someone might misunderstand your heading;

- simplifications for people for whom English is a second language;

- what the menu words sound like. Remember that the visually impaired may be using synthesized speech technology, so make sure the sound is unambiguous too.

Haiku is a minimalist poetic form—conveying a great deal in three short lines

You are not alone if you find these decisions difficult. It is like finding *le mot juste* for a poem. It can be easier to write 1000 words of straight text.

The table on p. 103 shows some of the different expectations people have when they look round a site trying to contact someone directly. You can see from that how much room for misunderstanding there is. Every menu word counts.

If the menus are graphics buttons, provide text-based links as well and use the ALT tag to give the menu name. Some people still have slow Internet access and choose not to download images. And partially sighted users, who can use their browser settings to increase the font size, may not be able to read the graphic versions of the menus since these are unaffected by browser text settings.

Titles and headings

A web page has several levels of heading that guide the user through the content:

the title code	→	page name hidden from view in the source code
the page title	→	heading describing the subject of the page
section heads	→	headings to break up a long page
link headings	→	jump-links at the top or left side leading to subheadings

Title code

The title code looks like this and it is not necessarily the same as the page title. Let's imagine it's for the page you are reading now. One could put:

```
<title>Dorner: Writing for the Internet – Chapter 5: Titles and headings</title>
```

or just

```
<title>Titles and headings</title>
```

When someone comes to a website they would like to bookmark, the words within the <title> </title> code will appear in the Bookmark or Favourites listing. So you are giving more information to your user if you have a longer, explanatory title. They'll remember what the page was and why they saved the link. If you are writing for a company, putting their name first in the title code on every page can be useful PR and may increase the hits to that site.

The downside is that all page titles then start with the same letter of the alphabet so it's is harder for the writing team to find pages they need to edit in a contents listing. Using easily understood filenames may help that problem (.htm .html .phtml .asp and so on).

The canny web writers write mini-adverts, e.g.:

First Direct – the Internet Bank you can talk to

or

BBC Online – Audio and Video – the Best of Radio and TV Online

Page title

'Writing for the web is often writing to be found.'

Jakob Nielsen

The page title is what your users will see when they have clicked through from a menu choice. A mini-advert is not what they want. They want to absorb quickly and instantly what the page is about. Web writers can learn from newspapers where three styles of titles are common:

Information	Earthquake in India kills 90%
Witty	Gloom with a View
Intriguing	Hix Nix Vix Pix

The last is obscure—it translates as 'Mid-Western Farmers (Hicks), give a film about Queen Victoria (Vic's Pics) the thumbs down (Nix)'.

The double-meaning style of heading is popular in the UK. Sometimes this is effective; sometimes it gives rise to the sort of groan a pun often elicits.

The information heading is the one we want on a web page. A good page title is not a mini-advert, but a mini-story; who did what, and to whom. Boil down the facts so you are left with something that will let readers know they are on the right page.

Section headings

Long web pages (discussed above) are often broken up into digestible chunks separated by sub-headings. The heading works best if it is short, but descriptive. So

Improving e-books

is better than

A Few Things that Absolutely Must Change in the e-Book Industry

These are 'anchored' to the link headings with a code such as this:

```
<a name="improve">Improving e-books</a>
```

Link headings

Link headings are like tabloid newspaper cross-heads that catch the eye and guide readers to particular sections. People read newspapers non-sequentially too. It is commonly done on a web page with one-word headings that sum up the paragraph to which they refer and click-link the reader down to it. They can be shortened versions of section headings. So, using the example above,

| improvements |

Note the vertical slash known as a pipe mark (|), which has no function in everyday text. On the Internet it separates items on the same line in a link list at the top or left-hand side of the screen. The coding for that would be

```
<a href="#improve">improvements</a>
```

and jumps the reader down to see what all those things that absolutely must change the e-book industry are.

Writing hyperlinks

Links are really only electrified contents pages, footnotes, cross-references, or indexes. With the exception of some (few) original creative writing experiments, there is almost nothing the Internet adds to informational text that does not occur in the book or magazine world. It's simply a more convenient way of jumping about. That's all hyperlinking is on most websites.

Signalling contents

The sections, departments, subject areas, or themes forming the major divisions of the site are like chapters. You can represent them as graphics or plain text. They should appear on the entry page to the site and on every other page. The convention is in a row at the top or in a column on the left, repeated in text-only form at the foot of very long pages. This developed out of browser limitation, but conventions are useful, as the eye knows where to look.

These link phrases are not meaningful

Click here to Enter
Click on this
Select this
Current information

Be consistent and use the same wording on every page. So don't put How to join on one page and Sign up on another. And use a design feature so visitors always know where they are in the site.

It is generally not helpful to have a Previous / Forward pair of hyperlinks. You do not know where your user has come from. Remember that it is very annoying for the user to click through several screens to reach a desired target. Try to think how you can organise the structure so this does not happen.

Footnoting

Don't put too many links within the text. You want your reader to stay with you to absorb your point, not dash off somewhere else because there's a link. So try to keep lists of links in one place – elsewhere on the page as 'see also' material or even on a separate links page. When it *is* useful to embed a link to extra information in the text, keep the link words as short as possible

(2–4 words only) so the eye can instantly absorb them. And try to give readers some idea of what they will find.

See comparative <u>rainfall statistics</u> for 1999 and 2001.

is better than

<u>Click here</u> for more about the rainfall statistics.

It is safe to assume that the reader will understand that underlining indicates a hyperlink. 'Click here' is becoming redundant. The convention is to use blue for the link and purple for a visited link – that's a design decision, and audiences are sophisticated enough now to adapt to any colour.

Link titles

To keep sentence length to a minimum, use link titles. Try:

See <u>rainfall statistics</u>.

The title code gives a brief description of what readers can expect if they click on the link and appears as hover text when the user rests the cursor on the link. See the box for the HTML code.

```
See <a href="stats.htm"
title="comparative details
for 1999 and 2001">rainfall
statistics</a>
```

Use this sparingly, as it puts the onus on the reader to hover over the link and is yet another thing to do. It also slows the loading of the page (only fractionally). Ten words of title code is more than enough. Information to use in a link title includes:

■ name of the site if it is not the current one;

■ warnings if a page is password-protected;

■ descriptive detail you don't want to put in the text subdirectory if the site has a complex tree structure.

Bullets and lists

Bullets look good on screen and are useful aids to clarity because the eye grows weary reading across the screen. In print, too many lists get tedious; on screen they act as a cosmetic aid. Nested lists can convey information quickly. Good uses of lists include:

- to itemise a genuine list
  - recommendations of a report;
  - features of a product;
  - catalogues;
  - price lists.

- Main points or executive summary.

- To itemise a set of examples or anecdotes.

- Series of hyperlinks to other resources.

- Document archives (in .PDF or other format).

One of the principles of the web is to save people's time.

Here and now

The web is here and now, so use immediate language.

Be active

Use active verbs in the present tense. So instead of:

> A lot of comments were received by us.

Say .

> We receive a lot of comments.

Be positive

Always be up-beat. If you say:

> Due to the high number of comments we receive, we can't respond to every email.

it makes your respondent feel 'why bother?' It's better to say:

> We read customers' comments with interest, even though we cannot respond individually. Thank you for helping us make this a better site.

Two-way communication improves websites and client relationships

Be direct

> Go to the clubs to make friends, have fun, and learn.

is easier to understand than:

> If you want to make friends and you are a fun-loving sort of person who likes learning, then click on the club button at the top of the page.

6 Web nuts and bolts: editing

Chapters 4 and 5 explored some of the decisions a writer needs to make when planning and drafting the text for each page in a website. This chapter looks at the equally time-consuming task of revising. Some people write and rewrite as they go along— Flaubert used to speak of combing a sentence till it shines. Others get it all down, put it aside to rest, and then review the whole lot, red pencil in hand. Some rely on an editor to rewrite. See the roles chart on p. 11 if you are part of a team.

The writer needs to bow down to the household god of editing: Consistency. Copy-editing isn't prized on the Internet, so the writer must fulfil that nit picky role. It's all to do with getting the message across and making sure the reader understands. The site visitor irritated by a typo, ambiguity, PR-speak, or inconsistency is not a well-disposed reader. Of course, it's hard to monitor, as the web is a dynamic medium, and consistency choices made on a previous update are easy to forget.

Being self-critical

It is easier to edit someone else's text than your own. Somehow one can see, with blinding clarity, how a few small structural changes will make the flow of an argument clear: but look at your own, and you can't see the wood for the trees.

You get fond of words or phrases that you want to keep and get offended when others don't appreciate them. You don't even see your own spelling mistakes. These are called literals in the trade, which is a kind way of saying that of course it's the keyboard that can't spell, not you.

In an ideal world, everyone needs an editor, someone who comes fresh to the writing and sees the strengths and faults with clarity. Even if you have a third eye, you should still learn to read your own work critically and do as much editing as you can yourself.

A rough rule of thumb is that editing takes 10–15% of writing time. So remember to allow for that when you are working to a deadline. Estimates are within this range for online pages of 300–500 words:

Substantial edit including rewriting	1–2 pages per hour
Copy edit	4–6 pages per hour
Light edit	8–10 pages per hour

There are many excellent reference books to help with knotty points of language and grammar. What follows in this chapter is supplementary to those: editing points that apply in a particular way to writing for the Internet.

Here are some starting points:

Cross out:

a last paragraph if it reads as a conclusion (and put it first)

useless adjectives

long or unfamiliar words

clichés (like ... 'and that's official', 'alive and well', 'trouble flared when', 'over the moon')

exclamation marks (unless the text says 'Good God!' ... or equivalent) and never allow two of them

any personal opinion in formal writing

Then:

cut sentences of over 25 words into two.

change the passive voice to active 'he picked up the book' not 'the book was picked up'

turn round negative sentences like 'not for nothing did they ...'

turn round inversions, e.g. 'found to be effective was ...'

Use adjectives sparingly on a web page. They should not raise questions in the reader's mind, it should answer them. 'Sea-green' informs. 'Tall' invites the question: how tall?

Electronic editing

There is no such thing as automatic editing, of course, but you can use word-processor routines for the following:

- Search and replace to achieve consistency, e.g. e-mail or email, on-line or online (both are acceptable, and one strong view is that when a word goes into general usage there is no longer any need to hyphenate, hence 'email' but 'e-book').

- Word count to monitor your preferred page length.

- Grammar and spelling checker as a first 'throw' at weeding out errors (you will have to read intelligently as well); I prefer to run this *after* the first draft as I find it distracting to have the checkers running as I type.

- Check your readability. If this is part of the grammar checking in your word-processor, you can deselect all the options so the program only looks for readability statistics.

Tip:
Get to know your word-processor in detail: some functions can save a great deal of time.

- Turn on Track Changes if you want to show others what alterations you have made, or if you need to review changes made by another reader on the document you are working on. In Microsoft Word this is in the Tools menu; other programs may call this function Edit Trace, Document Comparison, or Redlining.

- Autocorrect standard errors on the fly, such as common mistypings, like 'teh' or 'abuot', or 'adn'. Add your own, or use this function as a short cut to longer phrases.

- Replace double hyphens with an en-dash or em-dash, and replace straight quotes with 'smart' quotes; this is better done in the word-processor if you are planning to block-copy the text into a graphical web-creation package as many of them handle dashes and quotation marks very poorly (see pages 58, 59, and 83 for details).

- Make sure you get a *right* single quote in omissions such as 'in the '90s'. Your word-processor will get this wrong, so block-copy the correct mark from the end of the numeral and paste it in front. Note: 90's is wrong.

Macros

Macros come in many guises and can be very useful for tailoring to company needs, or for stringing together routines for searching and replacing according to House Style.

A good macro can be adapted for any other project, so a little time spent in initial problem-solving can pay off very quickly. The trick is to avoid spending more time working out how to do something automatically than you would have done if you had plodded on manually. Make sure you will use it regularly (and remember its name).

To subscribe to an e-zine that gives tips on automated editing routines go to:

The word 'macro' derives from 'macro-instructions' – originally a long, list of instructions for a compiler in the early days of computing

<http://www.vitalnews.com/WordTips>

A macro that counts your word frequency—giving a sorted list of every word in the document and the number of times you have used it—is surprisingly useful for showing individuals their own stylistic quirks.

You can do a certain amount of editing on screen, but always, always print it out and read it on paper before you publish to the Internet. As discussed in Chapter 2, all the standards developed for traditional print apply on the Internet too.

Editing for sense

Computers are not human beings and they have much less information about a sentence than the writer. So although it helps to use built-in style-checkers, they are only a first throw at finding mistakes. You need to read for sense.

Certain types of error will not succumb to computer analysis. And web writers, because they are often technologically sophisticated, tend to forget this. This page spread offers a selection of badly put together sentences that require intelligent reading. These are types of error frequently found on the Internet.

Dangling phrases

You need to determine whether the subject of a phrase is the same as the nearest available subject to judge whether it is dangling or not. Compare these sentences:

Walking down the street, the clock in the tower struck noon.

Walking down the street, the girl in the red skirt stubbed her toe.

You need to know that girls can walk the streets and clocks cannot to recognize the error. A similar example of starting with the wrong bit of the sentence leads to 'back-to-frontery', as in:

Strapped to her thigh, the customs officer found a packet of heroin.

What (or who) was strapped to her thigh?

Ambiguity

The way in which you place words in the sentence can lead to ambiguity. Look at these two sentences:

> The student learnt to type quickly.
> The student quickly learnt to type.

The word 'quickly' is an adverb and its position in the sentence shows which word it emphasizes. But an adverb may refer to what precedes it or what follows. Because it looks two ways it is sometimes called a 'squinter':

> Drinking normally doesn't upset me.

This could have two meanings, so you would want to rephrase it to make the meaning clear.

> Normally, drinking doesn't upset me.

or

> Normal drinking doesn't upset me.

Ambiguity comes from uncertainty about emphasis, as in the sentence:

> Are they cooking apples?

Spelling checkers are useful, but not for words that are correctly spelled but used wrongly. These are called 'confusibles' or 'confusables' and include:

bred	bread	
cite	site	sight
I	eye	aye
it's	its	
red	read	
slay	sleigh	
their	there	they're
too	two	to
your	yore	you're
wet	whet	

This could mean are they (some people) cooking apples, or are they (the apples) cooking kinds of apples. When you're writing you have to think how other people might misunderstand what you are saying and try to phrase that so there is only one way of reading it.

Writing for the web is no different from other types of writing, but because readers have less time to absorb the message, it is doubly important to consider how it may be misunderstood. You owe it to your reader to make your meaning clear. If the reader might get the wrong mental image, then think how you can rephrase your sentence.

Redundancy

Official web writing has lots of redundancy in reports, white papers, insurance policies, and so on. People still think that if they can drag in lots of obscure, clever, or fashionable words, arranged in long, involved sentences, with lots of sub-clauses, and pauses for breath (like this one), then the reader will think them frightfully bright and will think they must know what they are talking about. Not so—onscreen readers want to grasp what is being said; and quickly too. So give them bread and butter and leave the canapés with radish flowers, twirls of lemon, and flags on sticks for some other occasion.

Experiment

Try this. Take a piece of white paper and cover the bottom half of any heading on this page. Like this:

Understanding

Official web writing contains redundancies. People think long sentences prove knowledge. They don't. Onscreen readers want to grasp the gist. So give them the facts; and quickly too.

You can still read that, can't you? So perhaps there is more information in the formation of a word on a page than the eye needs. Now go through a paragraph and white out all the vowels with some tippex; you can still read that too, though it may not be particularly comfortable. Now try reducing the first paragraph of this section (105 words) to a third (as in the box).

Unnecessary words

In shortening a piece of work, it's often quickest to précis the original—to abstract the sense without losing meaning. You can also delete words that add nothing. As in these examples:

When did they meet *up*?
Be careful next time *round*.
This moment in *time*.
They have a *mutual* dislike of *each other*.
These are *trivial* matters of *no importance*.

It is not impressive to use words like 'condition', 'situation', 'state', or 'factor' which people sometimes use to add tone. Look at the fragments below and consider whether they are adding anything at all to the meaning:

In bad weather (conditions)…
We had to accept the risk (factor)

Other words to edit out are descriptive words that add nothing at all to the noun they are describing, such as:

very unique

new innovation

past history

informal chat

great majority

high degree of perfection

> An American University has an annual contest to banish words or phrases from English for 'misuse, overuse, and general uselessness'.
>
> What do you think of the nominations in the box?

Repetition

Repetition is not *necessarily* redundancy. You might want the same information on a page (links, for example) presented in different ways. Readers use different strategies for finding what they want, so your aim is to help them do that. Once a reader finds something in one place on a page, they often will continue to look at the same area of the screen on other pages.

So menu choices shown as graphic buttons could appear again as text options at the foot of a page as well as in a drop-down information box or as an in-text link. The question for writers is whether to use the same form of words each time, or to use a synonym or different phrasing to catch the attention of a different audience. You may get more hits to a page by labelling it in different ways. Or you may irritate users because they have come to the same page twice thinking it offered something different.

know what I'm saying

thinking outside the box

cybrarian

digerati

24/7

feathers really flew

and that's official

vivacious

writing on the wall

double whammy

netizen

millionerd

marketroid

Punctuation marks

Here's an old school favourite, intended to amuse us and to illustrate the importance of punctuation:

> King Charles walked and talked half an hour after his head was cut off

And copy-editors regularly come up with examples of how costly the omission of a comma can be, as in:

> The demolition team should retain Drem station bridge and signal box.

They demolished Drem station. A comma after the word 'station' would have prevented that.

If readers have to reread a sentence several times because it isn't clear, then that can be expensive too. They might go to another site and yours will lose a customer. Or think of the amount of downtime there is in a company if all staff waste even a few seconds wrestling with meaning. Punctuation shows where the pauses are in texts and helps us understand the sense and flow of a piece.

Showing on screen

The Internet has not got a good track record for caring about punctuation. It is changing now. And, in turn, it is having an impact on the marks we use. Internet-writing may change some niceties. For example:

■ Dashes and slashes show up better on the screen than a combination of dots and are being used more frequently. You may no longer need to distinguish between colons and semi-colons in web writing.

■ Brackets are changing shape: it is easier for non-typists to use square brackets because they are on the lower shift of a computer keyboard.

■ Foreign accent setting is achieved with difficulty on screens. The chances are that words that are accepted as English, such as cliché, will lose their accents.

> The HTML code for a left single quote is ‘
>
> A right single quote or apostrophe is ’
>
> A smart left double quote is “
>
> A right double quote is ”
>
> single hyphen - (no special code needed)
>
> en-dash – (coded as –) or em-dash — (coded as —)
>
> a double hyphen -- looks amateurish and it is worth spending a little extra time trying to get this right.
>
> Typographers use thin spaces before and after an en-dash (not achievable in HTML) and no spaces on each side of an em-dash

■ Smart quotes and apostrophes (i.e. proper 6 and 9 shapes as shown on p. 59) can be difficult to code, but the straight prime mark offends the discerning eye. Single quotes are standard for UK style and also look better on web pages.

■ The dreadful multiple exclamation mark is everywhere on the Internet. It's either because insecure writers do not know what it is for (see p. 108) or because humour on the screen needs flagging up.

■ Plain text in emailed newsletters is developing a brand of different keypad combinations to draw the attention— *word* or _word_ both indicate italics. This may develop.

■ Other punctuation marks are coming into usage in email and e-zines, not to separate sentences into understandable parts, but as attention-seekers to make headings stand out or to separate paragraphs, e.g.:

>>> About My Company <<<
****** {-} ******
= = = = = = = = = = = =

New punctuation marks

~ tilde

hash

/ slash

\ backslash

| pipe

_ underscore

. dot

House style

British style is always day-month-year. Preferably 1 June 2002, not 1st June 2002 or June 1, 2002.

Correct phone style is: +44 (0)20 7123 4567 not (+44) 0207 123 4567

Numerals are easier to take in on a website – so step 1: not step one:

Styling of dates and numbers is another issue—see the box for details.

See also the House style checklist on pp. 110–11.

For that matter, is it 'email', 'e-mail', or 'Email'? What about 'online' or 'on-line'; is 'website' one word or two? And what format do you use for URLs, domain names, and email addresses? Or, how do you treat site and page names when they appear in text? Can you use 'dot-com' or 'ftp' as a *verb*? This book uses both.

These are decisions you will have to make as you edit the entire text on the site. There are no correct forms for the new words of the Internet. Indeed, many other words have alternative spellings and it is the editor's job to decide what spellings to use. This is called house style and the golden rule here is that Consistency is king.

You can be consistent in many ways. The *Oxford English Dictionary* advisory team says *e* is the hot prefix in English, generating new word forms nearly every day, such as e-cash, e-zine, e-book, e-banking. There are almost too many '*e*'s about. You can decide that consistency demands that you hyphenate the lot. Or you can decide that once a word has earned its bread (as email has) then the e- prefix is obsolete. It doesn't stand for 'electronic mail'; it's now 'email'.

Spelling and usage dictionaries will give you the correct and alternative forms of some disputed words, but below are a number that are particular to web writing. Many are waiting to 'settle'; that is to say, there is a lot of freedom and we wait to see how language is used in the e-medium.

The coordinating writer should draw up a list of words that apply to their own organisation—every company will have different lists—and circulate them round the writing team.

Word list

back up (verb), backup (noun and adj)	full-scale	offline
	HTMLing (verb)	offscreen
bandwidth	Internet or internet	online
Ccing and CC'd (for copied to)	jpeg (in text) .jpg (as part of a filename)	onscreen
centring on (not around, not centering)	keyword	part-time
		print-out (noun), print out (verb)
chatroom or chat room	laptop	pulldown (adj)
co-operate	listserv (not listserve)	realtime
co-ordinate	log off (verb), logoff (adj)	re-use
desktop (noun and adj)	log on (verb), logon (adj)	rework
dial in	MB or Mb	rewrite
dial up (verb), dialup (adj)	MHz	screensaver
disc (for CD-ROMs, DVDs)	mouseclick, mouseover, mousepad	screenshot
disk (for hard drives and floppies)	MPEG (in text) .mpg (as part of a filename)	spellcheck (noun and verb), spellchecker
downtime		start-up
dpi (for dots per inch)	multi-task or multitask	toolbar
e- prefix for all sorts of things	multi-user or multiuser	typeface
e-commerce	net (for network)	user name or username or user ID
e-zine or webzine or zine	Net (for Internet)	
FAQ (not FAQs)	netiquette	user or member or reader or ...
fast-track	multimedia	voicemail or voicemail
filename or file name	multi-purpose	webmaster or web editor
ftp'd and ftp'ing (verb)	newsgroup	website or web site or Web site

Simple language

Simple language:

– reduces ambiguity
– speeds reading
– is more understandable for non-English readers
– makes automatic translation easier

Simple language is more accessible. It is also better because of the inherent difficulties of reading from screens (explored in more detail on p. 26).

Simplified English is a useful model. It has developed in many forms, particularly in the aerospace industry, where safety is paramount and where use of synonyms can lead to fatal misunderstandings. It consists of a limited vocabulary (where a family of synonyms is represented by one of its members) and sets of writing rules.

Words are chosen for their simplicity as well as their relationship to other languages; for example, 'occur' is more international than 'happen'. The box has a small selection of alternative suggestions in the Simplified English dictionary.

There is no need to use anything that does not sound right, but remember that the Internet is global. Should English-speakers expect the world to change; or should they bend towards what the world can understand more easily?

accessible – get access to	detect – find	inoperative – is off
achieve – get	develop – start, make, cause	liable – that can
acknowledge – tell	discontinue – stop	mend – repair
activate – start, operate	enforce – must	mention – give
allocate – give	enlarge – make larger, increase	mistake – error
allow – let, permit	envisage – think	motion – movement
approach – go near	evaluate – make an analysis	nearly – almost
assign – give	execute – do	notify – tell
assume – think	facilitate – help, make easier	obtain – get
combine – mix	feature – shape, property, quality, different	preferable – better, possible, recommend
commence – start		
communicate – tell	final – last	simply – easily, only
conform – agree	identical – same	transform – change
conventional – usual	implement – do, make	utilize – use

Quoting and referencing

The same rules of citation apply to research material found on the Internet as anywhere else. The format you use depends on the discipline of your own subject area and will match the bibliographical styles (e.g. the academic conventions of the Harvard, Chicago, MLA, APA styles and many more). All are different in detail, but the following principles apply to quoting web-originated materials.

■ Make sure a reader can find the source you are citing.

■ The citation for a web document often follows a format similar to that for print, with some information omitted and some added.

■ If you cannot find some elements of information, cite what *is* available, e.g.:
   ○ Instead of a title, there may only be a file name.
   ○ The place of publication and the name of the publisher may be replaced online by the URL.

■ If the work was originally created for print, it may be necessary to give the date of the original print publication.

■ Online authors may only use login names or aliases.

■ Always include the date that you accessed the source (equivalent to the edition).

■ Cite the complete address (URL) accurately (within angled brackets is the MLA style). Include the access mode (http, ftp, telnet, etc.). If you have to divide the URL between two lines, break only after a slash mark and do not insert a hyphen at the break.

■ URLs do, unfortunately, change. Researchers generally realize that they may have to step back to the core domain name in a URL that has several directory layers.

See also online reference information in Part B, p. 116.

Legalese

Web editors should avoid editing any legal documents that are on the site, as these are always carefully crafted by lawyers. You may sometimes want to change anything that is not in your own house style (e.g. capitalizations) but avoid adding commas, as legalese tends to have its own reasons for allowing for the possibility of ambiguity.

On a corporate site, significant new content on the web pages should be seen at least twice by department heads, other key people, and internal auditors and lawyers. Ideally, all the group's managing directors should approve key sections before the site goes live.

The site editor will be responsible for making sure this vetting process occurs. Check which of the following legal documents the site should have:

- Credits and permissions

- Copyright statement

- Disclaimers

- Privacy statements

- Terms and conditions of use

- E-commerce encryption assurances

- Statutory rights

Some details are in Part B, pp. 112–4, but ask a lawyer.

Indexing

Indexing is a special skill. A usable index requires considerable knowledge and imaginative thinking. These are qualities a computer does not have. Yet on websites, computer-indexing is rife. For a start, most search engines that do an internal search of the site are computer-generated. So you might want to add a topic-based index on an information-rich site to help your visitors navigate. These points may be helpful:

■ Search engines use ASCII numbering as the basis of sorting, and this is not consistent with international standards (e.g. ISO 999 or BS 3700). For example, anything appearing in single quotation marks would come towards the top of the index (because an open quote is ASCII value 96 and the letter 'a' is 97), whereas the open quote should be ignored. Similarly, 'database' would always come after 'data systems' because the space character is ASCII value 32 and therefore comes before 'b', which is 98.

■ ASCII sorting also does not take into account that leading prepositions, articles, and conjunctions should not form part of an alphabetical sort: word-processor indexing would probably put 'The Quiet Games' under 'T' instead of 'Q'. Ignored, too, are standard rules about abbreviations, e.g. that 'St Anne' should be alphabetized as if it were spelled in full as 'Saint Anne'.

■ There are countless problem areas that require human intelligence and knowledge. For example, an index entry for a peer of the realm not only requires human interaction in how the names are to appear (family name first or hereditary title), but also a logical decision where alphabetical and numerical sorting are at variance (should the 6th Earl with the first name of Angus appear before the 1st Earl who is called Zebedee?).

■ In order to subdivide entries, there needs to be some analysis of the text, gathering together related information, cross-referring to synonyms, and so on. Computers cannot do this.

■ Automatic systems do not usually distinguish between singulars and plurals, so a consistent decision needs to be made when editing.

■ The search engine will not distinguish between an abbreviation and a word or phrase. So 'deoxyribonucleic acid; DNA; nucleic acid; nucleic acids' would come up as separate entries: users prefer a consolidated one.

The one area in which the Internet scores is cross-referencing and footnoting. Both work more neatly than book indexing: through hypertext links.

Tip:
Understanding how computers index helps define strategies when using Internet search engines.

7 | Website genres

Romance, horror, thrillers, essays, news stories, literary novels, and so on are all different writing genres. Each has its own conventions that readers accept. A convention in detective fiction, for example, is the denouement at the end where all the threads of the suspense are tied up and the identity of the murderer revealed. Not all detective fiction follows that formula (how dull it would be if every story were the same) but readers are comfortable when they know what to expect.

Websites also fall into a number of genre patterns, and some of the most obvious are analysed in this chapter. In all cases visitors want to know at first glance:

■ what will be in the main areas of a site;

■ what the naming conventions stand for;

■ how to move around the site;

■ where they are in it.

Get these right and you are already half-way to having a successful site. So if you didn't read the section on evaluating other sites in Chapter 3 (pp. 38–41), turn back to it now because it is all about what to look out for.

You'll also see that the various types of site in this chapter rely on your knowing who your readers are and what the conventions of similar sites are.

There are dozens of web genres to fit every different interest group. They cover personal sites, clubs and societies, corporate sites, intranets, university and information venues, search engines, special subject portals, courses and training, international projects, as well as banking, auction rooms, and online shopping.

The next few pages look at the details of three main genres:

■ **personal home pages**
→ because many readers of this book may want to start by writing for a personal site for self-advertising

■ **brochure-ware**
→ because people in the workplace all need to consider whether the Internet is suitable for publicity materials

■ **community sites**
→ because this is another obvious starting point for those who run clubs, societies, and local or virtual special interest groups

Some sites are static, which means that once the content is right it can sit on the site indefinitely. If time or funding is limited, this can be a good way of having a web presence without too much anxiety. It's best to keep date-related material to a minimum.

Others are interactive, which means they need constant monitoring and sophisticated technology driving the way the content is displayed. Depending on the size of the venture, this may mean setting aside half a day a week for updating, or it may require teams of full-time employees.

The Greek philosopher Plato thought people should not encounter ideas in the form of your 'textual self' without meeting you.

He spoke against books – what would he have thought about web pages?

Plato lived in the fifth century BC, when very few people could read and write.

Personal home pages

There has never before been such a wide-reaching personal publishing medium. Everyone can present a 'virtual self' to the world. There is seldom a profiteering motive, simply some underlying desire to assert one's identity in a global setting.

Personal home pages tend to follow a pattern which include these main menu choices:

About me	My interests	Things I do	Things I like	Where else to go	Contact me

The elements normally include:

- a welcome page;

- biographical statements, CV, and picture;

- about home, family, friends (pets), and region;

- likes and dislikes (media preferences, collections, travel, sports, interests) or ideas, beliefs and causes (religious, political, philosophical);

- samples of original work (published or unpublished writings, photographs, animations);

- links to other similar people or groups;

- a message board or real time chat room;

- an email link.

If you have never created a set of web pages before, this is a good place to start. Try writing a 50-word 'welcome' message about yourself. Write four different versions.

1 to appeal to friends and family;
2 to appeal to a prospective client;
3 as the beginning of story;
4 to focus on a special interest.

Consider which works best and what set of clickable options you want to offer next. Write them down, in any order, and then try to boil down the choices to six options.

Learn from other people. How do these two (fairly typical) examples of an opening page impress you?

1.

Hi and welcome to the entrance into my house! I have had some graphix difficulties due to a fault in my computer, and that is why I have no graphix on this page. Sorry! I finally managed to get my homepage up and running, so you can visit it now.

2.

It all began in 1966 after a lot of pushing, sweat and pain, out I popped. "It's a boy!" they shouted. I can't remember too much about that, but I've seen some photographs to confirm the incident.

Remember that your reader will not miss what is not there. So if (as in no. 1. above) you decide to have a text-only site, do not apologize; make a virtue of it. Take conscious spelling choices. Perhaps the writer felt 'graphix' rather than 'graphics' expresses humour. No. 2. above is self-expression—nothing wrong with that if other people are going to be as interested as the writer. Ask yourself how long you would stay at this site.

Successful personal profiles will:

■ engage the visitor because there is a shared interest;

■ indicate what is on the other pages;

■ have up-to-date personal data;

■ have static pages that do not need changing too often.

Writing focus for personal home page:

Presenting yourself well
Constructing a good CV

CV

If you hope to attract employers, then the CV page is the one to concentrate on. Have it all on one page with a 'contents' line at the top showing a range of achievements so the reader can jump straight to the relevant one, e.g.:

Recent work I Experience I Media I Education I Memberships I Awards
↘ link to section

| # Interactive brochures

Small companies and self-employed people can benefit greatly from having a 24-hour Internet presence. It is cheaper than a paper booklet, always instantly available, and clients can browse quietly without anyone's knowledge.

For those who cannot afford the high maintenance and cost of fully-fledged e-commerce sites, a simple suite of pages that replace, or supplement, a brochure is enough for clients to get a sense of what the company, or individual, does and whether it is worth making further contact.

An online handout—known as 'brochureware'—might be the first contact a potential customer has with you. First impressions count for a great deal. Obviously the design is paramount. It's the words, however, that carry the information.

Rule number one. Do not build an Internet presence from documents created for print—brochures, PR material, and so on. They are always written in advertising-speak, and reviewing committees often make it worse. It's very, very difficult to make those committees see that what they have agreed for print just will *not* translate to the web. In fact the texts need a great deal of editing and much thought.

reduce to 1 short web page = 250 words

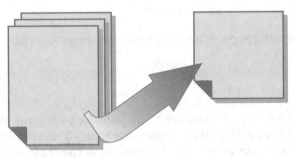

3 pages of text = 1000 words

Keep the brochure texts for reference, but start again from scratch. Frankly, your committee may think company history is very important and would probably put it in a prominent position in a booklet. But the web is interactive: users decide the page order now. If you don't think they really care about company history (and why should they?) then bury it on a second level somewhere within the site. After all, if you have information for the public then it might as well be available. If a visitor decides to take up what's on offer, they may then look for credentials.

If you can refine what the company or person does to three distinct areas and write 300 words about each one, then you are doing well. That's not a rule, but try it as an exercise.

Every business concern will have its own requirements. A furniture-maker, for example, may only need a personal statement; pictures and descriptions of the furniture made; and a price list. That is all a potential buyer cares about. Other details can follow on request.

Consider fitting the main menu choices into this type of form:

Welcome	Products or Services	How to buy
Company history	What's new	Search
FAQ	Archive	How to find us

Opening screen

The term 'Home page' is beginning to acquire a slight pejorative tinge—it tends to mean a personal home page. A company opening screen is like the cover of book and combined contents page. It should have a clear title, credits, simple and clear graphics, and top-level links to the inside pages. Above all, it needs a strap line. Your visitor should know at a glance what the company does and what the site offers.

You may also decide to feature news or special promotions on the opening page to bring traffic back to the site. Some people use animated scripting or tickertape text for this because it gets more words onto the front page. But it's kind to make sure that people who find animations irritating can turn them off.

Communities

An online or virtual community is a gathering of people in an online 'space' where they connect, communicate, and get to know each other better using the Internet. They can be clubs, societies, or gatherings of people who come together for a common interest. Main menus vary, but usually include:

About the community	Members	How to join	Sub-groups	Forum	News & Events	Search	Info

It works best if there is a 'leading light', someone who wants to make the community happen. That is almost always the person who will be writing for all the others. Online communities and virtual work-groups do not always 'happen' spontaneously. They often require care and nurturing: facilitation. That can range from goading other people into offering contributions to deciding how to post them up for others to see.

Each community will be what you and your members make of it; everyone in it has a personal responsibility to make it succeed. And it will if there is a genuine sense of purpose, ownership, and audience with shared aims, goals, and interests. Participants need to feel they can *and want* to make the time to use it.

So honing communication skills becomes a way of influencing others. You can experiment with ways of writing that will influence, report, inform, or question. The steps it takes to set up a community generally follow this pattern.

■ Identify your community purpose—having a clear focus will help to give participants what they want.

■ Decide who can join and who will be a part of the community.

■ How will people introduce themselves in the community? It may be helpful to provide the community members with a template or framework to produce their own profile.

■ Start off with materials the group can relate to—keep it simple at the beginning.

■ Make decisions about your own role—how much control over the content you will have.

■ Make sure members understand how to behave online. You may need to produce some guidelines on 'netiquette' (see pp. 16–7).

■ Keep up the momentum. Set timescales for contributions to enable some things to finish whilst others are just starting. It keeps the community area fresh and interesting.

Writing focus for brochure-ware:

Putting across a strong message
Drawing visitors in
Making them act

Of all these, the last is probably the most challenging. Community leaders (offline as well as online) foster member interaction, provide stimulating material for conversations, keep the space cleaned up, and help hold the members accountable to their own guidelines.

As the writer and editor, you will be the one providing leadership, giving the community a focus, stimulating group interaction, offering support, team-building, refereeing, dealing with problems, timekeeping and responding to member feedback.

<http://www.gridclub.com/>

You can also divide the main space into smaller sub-communities and help community members do these things for themselves. It is all too easy for an online space to get sidetracked, disrupted, or simply abandoned. You can save yourself a great deal of aggravation if you are aware of these possibilities at the outset.

8

Keeping readers

Everything you have read so far is only stage one. It's the easy bit. Now the real work begins—and that is why, on p. 36, this book asked if you really need a website. You have to be fluid and keep the site alive so people want to come back. Write and rewrite constantly.

Maintenance

Users want up-to-date information. This has considerable resource implications and requires a great deal of energy from the person or department responsible for the site. And faster approval systems where top management has to pass the copy for 'press' (we lack a word here). Maintaining a website is a service industry. Do you need to look at it:

- hourly
- daily
- weekly
- monthly
- half-yearly?

Yearly is not an option unless the whole site is filled with completely static materials that will not change. A good rule of thumb is to allow one third of the total cost of a website for annual maintenance as the lowest starting point.

So if it cost £12,000 from initial 'dot-com-ing', then reckon on £4,000 for upkeep on a low-volume site and £12,000 for a high-maintenance site.

Keeping the site fresh

A fresh and successful site is known in the trade as 'sticky'—
your audience will stick with it. One of the difficulties is that
the Internet is primarily text-based. Yes, everyone uses images,
and audio and video are getting better, but the reality (as this
book has already made clear) is that the word is all-important.

So writing with care and clarity is paramount (it cannot be said
too often). Don't join the band of the bland—sites that look and
read as if they had no personality.

Here are some ideas:

- Feature something daily; and make it interesting. Give the
  casual visitor some prominent reason to click.

- Offer something free as an attraction for a site relying
  on sales. One company attracts subscribers by posting up
  sports scores.

- Write pieces that will appeal to your audience—and don't
  leave them at the top of the page for months at a time.
  Try new topics, and vary them so visitors can be engaged
  or re-engaged.

- 'Sell' online discussion by spelling out the benefits. Initiate
  group interaction—a debate, a discussion, a competition, a
  list of favourite 'somethings'.

- Respond to member feedback.

- Send out email alerts to tell people what's new.

- Encourage sub-groups (if it's a community site). Get new
  voices contributing and sharing ownership.

- Do housekeeping regularly—removing old material and
  dead links.

Supplementing the website

The trouble with the web is that people forget you are there. So keep reminding them. A good way to do this is to send out a newsletter or e-zine by email that draws them back to your site. Include a 'Subscribe' button on your site. Be careful, though, as there are so many of these now that recipients can get resentful if they didn't ask to receive them, so don't grab other people's lists and recirculate them. Remember too that there are data protection implications, so you need to reassure visitors that you are not passing on any details to any third party.

E-zines

E-zines arrive as plain ordinary text, so there are no design crutches to easy reading. You have to do it all using standard keyboard characters and spaces to draw attention to the headings. Here are some examples:

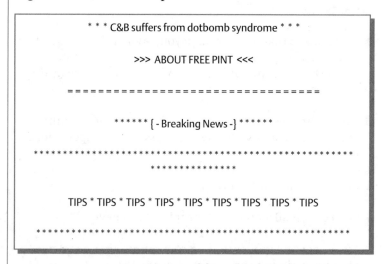

The advantage of an emailed e-zine is that you reach the customer or interested person directly, with no required effort on their part. But the reluctance to scroll applies to email text as well.

Write short, telling headlines that are compelling enough to send the reader clicking on the link to the full story. Or add a very short paragraph giving the highlights of the story. Here are some examples:

Security giant hit by hacker attack
<http://www.silicon.com/a42433>

Can Libraries Lead the Way?
Two-thirds of libraries in areas with populations of more than 500,000 people have purchased e-books for their systems.
<http://link.ixsl.net/s/link/click?rc=al&rti=427325&
si=ml0992552>

Publisher details

Don't forget to blow your own trumpet in the e-zine, e.g.:

ABOUT NUA
Nua is a leading provider of enterprise web publishing solutions in the knowledge management marketplace. Nua's customers are large organizations that want to create value and profit from their information and knowledge.
<http://www.nua.ie/products/index.shtml>

Include a copyright line in the e-zine:

Copyright 2002

All Rights Reserved. All broadcast, publication, retransmission, copying or storage is strictly prohibited without prior written permission from the publisher.

Each issue should let readers know how to unsubscribe, whether they can quote material, the circumstances under which they may forward the e-zine to other people, and how to contact a real person (see next page). You can also use the e-zine for survey questionnaires.

Customer contact

Every page should have a contact button unless there is a strong reason for burying this information deep within the site. A website that relies on fully automated routines, for example, may want to discourage individual contact because it is costly in personnel time to answer queries.

*Required Fields

**Your comment or question

**First name

**Last name

**Email address

We will use your email address for feedback purposes only.

See our Privacy Policy

It is annoying, however, for the user to hunt about looking for an email address or feedback form. The web editor can always choose to have automated systems for answering web-generated mail.

In the analogue world, customer care and individual attention are valued, and for many business uses the same still applies. So make it easy for your customers. If they get irritated, they will be reluctant to return to your site.

There are several ways of doing this. Have a button on a menu bar or as part of the footer to every page. Make sure it is always in the same position on every page in the web.

Consider your choice of wording carefully as your visitor may have different expectations from yours (see opposite). That is often why you need a profile of your intended audience so that you can second-guess how they will interpret quite simple wording. The possibilities in the table opposite show how difficult even such simple choices can be.

Feedback forms usually ask for minimal information from the user—name and email address at the very least. Demographic information is useful, but not all customers are willing to give it. Deciding what is required information (i.e. the user will not be able to submit the form without filling in fields marked *) is a marketing one; how you inform your user why you want it or what you will do next is a writing decision.

Naming of buttons

Button	Expectations
Email us	Pop-up email message form for a simple site Page listing appropriate people to email for a complex site
Contact us	Ambiguous; could be any of the described choices Names, telephone numbers, fax and physical address
Feedback	Form with scrolling box for comment on the site or the services and requests for some information about the user Possibility of email information also on the page
Help	List of choices, such as: Guide to site Password information How to find ... Anything listed below
Customer service	List of choices, such as: FAQ Technical advice How to ... information Policy statements Status of orders Anything listed above
Quiz or Competition	Disguised questionnaire to get customer profiling – works best if you offer a prize as incentive
Technical support	Support options
Media kit	Advertising details – often the only place on site where you can find addresses.

Tip:
When you set up the code to bring up an email message box add `?subject=` to the mailto: command to slot the subject into a message, e.g.

`mailto:sales@oup.co.uk?subject=Buy Jane Domer's book`

Part B
Contents

Good practice checklists

These checklists are for quick reference only. They are neither definitive nor exhaustive. They are simply reminders of the kinds of things to look out for. Use your own judgment; add others; cross out anything that does not suit your project.

Evaluating web content

Look for these things:

☐ a statement of the aims and objectives of the site;

☐ author and publisher details and an email link to back up authenticity;

☐ details of the origin of any data or information;

☐ mention of any quality checks or referencing of the information;

☐ creation and modification dates – age may or may not matter;

☐ clearly marked archival information;

☐ good design and awareness of readability—though many excellent academic papers scrawl in Courier head-to-toe across the screen;

☐ a sense of where you are on the site—not necessarily a site map, but some clear navigational hooks;

☐ a good search box—vital on an information-rich site.

In judging the content, ask yourself:

☐ Does the resource appear to be honest and genuine?

☐ Is the resource available in another format (e.g. a book or CD-ROM)?

☐ Do any of the materials infringe copyright?

☐ Is the information well researched?

☐ Is any bias made clear and of an acceptable level?

☐ Is it the result of a personal hobbyhorse?

☐ Is the information durable in nature?

☐ Is there adequate maintenance of the information content?

General writing

☐ Audience: know who you are writing for before you begin, and plan accordingly.

☐ Main points: hit your reader with the salient points at the top of the web page (people are reluctant to scroll). Use interior pages to unfold details and complexity.

☐ Be concise: cut every word that doesn't contribute. A good web-page length is under 300 words – it is better to divide anything longer than that into sub-topics.

☐ See pp. 50–53 for more detail about longer texts.

Be brief, but not bland.

☐ Write short paragraphs: paragraph breaks refresh the eye. Between 2 and 5 sentences is enough.

☐ Write simple sentences: ideas are easier to digest in a simple subject-verb-object progression. Make sub-clauses into separate sentences. Use one idea per sentence and keep sentences under 17 words (the average for print). Be brief, but not bland.

☐ Use the present or present perfect tense: the web is here and now. Keep passives away.

☐ Use specific words: 'red and blue' is better than 'multi-coloured'; 'snow and sleet' are better than 'bad weather'.

☐ Use plain words: 'began', 'said', 'end' rather than 'commenced', 'expressed', or 'terminated'.

☐ Be direct: the web is friendly. Use 'we' and 'you' instead of 'the insured', 'the applicant', 'the society', and so on.

☐ Be positive: 'the web works well' rather than 'the web doesn't function badly'.

☐ Spend time getting menu headings right: visitors may not understand where you are leading them.

☐ Filenames: it is safest to give short filenames like navig.htm rather than navigationonline.htm because some browsers do not recognize long names. Also, if you save a site to a CD-ROM, long filenames may get truncated—navigati~1.htm—and then none of the links will work.

☐ Page title: search engines often index under the page name, derived from the <Title> line, so give meaningful titles. Try not to leave your visitor thinking: 'Where am I, what's the name of this page?'

Editorial

☐ Consistency: as long as the whole site is internally consistent it does not matter what heading and spelling styles you choose.

☐ Spellcheck everything: people can be very cavalier about online spelling. It matters in print and it matters online. Good spelling is not an issue of correctness, but of consideration for the reader. It's best not to confuse or annoy readers: they won't attend to your message if you do.

☐ Read for sense on paper: automatic checking functions are useful, but do not do the job for you.

'Copy-editing is largely a matter of common sense in deciding what to do and of thoroughness in doing it.'

From Judith Butcher, *Copy-editing* (CUP, 3rd edn. 1992, ISBN: 0521400740)

☐ Cutting: strip out redundancies, repetition, verbosity, and jargon. No need to repeat questions in FAQ answers. Remember FAQ means Frequently Asked Questions so there is no need to add an 's' and make it FAQs.

☐ New visitors: delete or move material new visitors won't want to know. Make them feel at home before demanding registration (on a site that requests a login).

The interrobang was created in 1962 to fill a gap in our punctuation system where writers often used typographically cumbersome and unattractive combinations of the question mark and exclamation mark to punctuate rhetorical statements where neither the question nor an exclamation alone exactly served the writer, as in 'How about that?!'

☐ Exclamation marks: take them all out unless it's a true exclamation (like 'Oh dear!'). Get the designer to take them off the graphics buttons as well. If you want to indicate humour or irony, do it in a different way.

☐ Quotation marks: always single or, where necessary, double within single. Never use for titles. Use sparingly (preferably never) to give credence to a work that will not stand on its own.

☐ Apostrophes: not used before 's' when writing ISPs, 1990s, etc.

☐ Underlining: do not use underlining instead of italics; underlining is the convention for hyperlinking.

Will it catch on? You will find it on Microsoft fonts Wingdings 2.

☐ Dates and numbers: UK style is always day-month-year. Preferably 1 June 2002, not 1st June 2002 or June 1, 2002. It is best not to abbreviate dates because different conventions in the way this is done can lead to confusion. In the US the above date would abbreviate to 6/1/02; most other countries would write 1/6/02.

☐ Numerals (except for dates) are easier to take in on a website —so 'step 1', not 'step one'.

Phrases to avoid

These phrases are from the early days of the Internet; there is no need for any of them:

☐ 'Check it (or this) out'—make the reader want to continue.

- ☐ 'Click on the link'—make a meaningful link phrase instead.

- ☐ 'Site under construction'—sites are always dynamic and therefore never fully built.

- ☐ This site is best viewed using <browser and resolution specified> – if you must say it, tuck it away in the credits.

Text design

- ☐ Hyperlinks: check for usefulness as well as functionality. Try not to pepper the page with links; it confuses readers.

- ☐ Contact and help information to be always one click from any page.

- ☐ Colour: black text on white or cream backgrounds reads best. Avoid background patterning as it distracts the eye.

- ☐ Line length: constrained by the pixel width of a (hidden) table or column, but approximately 10–12 words per line, depending on the length of word.

- ☐ Alignment: left justified (also known as ragged right) is easier to read on screen than fully justified text.

- ☐ Display area: on low-resolution screens of 640 x 480 pixels, 535 pixels is the maximum text width for pages to print on standard A4 paper without cropping the text in the right hand column. This is entirely dependent on screen resolution and 800 x 600 or 1152 x 864 are now quite common. It depends on your intended audience.

- ☐ Use graphics sparingly: bullet points or graphic elements help pick out key words and concepts. But animations are irritating. Studies show that the message is lost when television images fail to reinforce spoken words. The same is true of the web.

House style

In addition to constructing a word list like the one on p. 85, decide a policy the following points of editorial consistency.

Text
Normal—preferably use a Cascading Style Sheet template.
No animated or blinking text

Spacing
1 space after a full stop.

Italics
Use for book titles, film titles, emphasis.
Avoid for body text. In emails decide between *title* and _title_

Quote marks
Single quotation marks, ' ' , to be used sparingly and set properly.

The more technically aware your readers are, the more quirky the links can be. For ease of understanding, the convention is a blue link word, underlined.

Links
Decide whether to:
—include the http:// protocol in listings
—show the full URL onscreen or whether to hide it behind the URL page title
—include the angle brackets in references < >

Use a consistent colour for links.
Underlining in links helps readers navigate.

Exclamation marks
Exclamation marks only for a genuine exclamation e.g. 'Oh dear!' not 'There are over 25,000 different orchids!'– but Yahoo! Because that is how the company spells it.

Capitalization

Capitals look worse on screens than on paper. In headings:

Decide on heading styles
or
Decide on Heading Styles
but not
Decide On Heading Styles
or
DECIDE ON HEADING STYLES

In company or product names, follow the company's own style:

PostScript
GeoCities
QuarkXPress
HotWired

but Nasdaq (although it is an acronym) need not be capitalized.

eBay, iMac and iVillage. Try to avoid beginning a sentence with these.

Intercaps such as 'aVANT-pOP' are for experimental sites.

Optional ftp or FTP; pdf or PDF; 'MUDs & MOOs' or 'muds and moos'—even though these derive from abbreviations.

Hyphenation

Follow a good spelling dictionary, but be prepared to close up words as they go into common usage, e.g. email not e-mail. The web mantra is 'save keystrokes'. Use hyphens for clarity, as in:

compound adjectives:	top-level domain name
onscreen command:	drag-and-drop
commands:	Control-Alt-Delete

Units of measure

Follow normal conventions. Typically, there is no space between them and the numbers: 600MHz, 1400dpi, 128k. MB and Mb have become optional, though Mb is technically correct.

Applicable law

This book can only give brief points and references. Always consult a lawyer.

Third party materials

Most web pages include links to third party materials. Shopping malls, online magazines, even simple pages with links to other interesting sites, will all include access to third party material. But users may not immediately realize what is your material and what is not, or even when they are leaving your site. It is sensible to make clear what is your material and what is third party material, and to ensure that you do not assume any responsibility that you would not otherwise have for the contents of third party material.

Under English law, if you link to third party material which is defamatory you may be liable for publishing it. It is unlikely that a disclaimer would make any difference to that, so think carefully about what you link to. Full details are on the Bird & Bird site <http://www.twobirds.com/library/internet/disc.htm>

Generally speaking, a simple link to another web site is not considered as infringement. However, when a link also contains a title and some text, infringement may take place and clearance is probably required. If you discover that a site to which you are linked is infringing copyright law you should break the link immediately. See <http://www.bodley.ox.ac.uk/scopin0g/appi.html>

Copyright

The laws of copyright apply to the Internet exactly as they do to print. Some details are on p. 36. For a full picture, see IP, the government-backed home of UK Intellectual Property on the Internet <http://www.intellectual-property.gov.uk/>

It is a good idea to have a copyright statement on your site with some wording like this:

> The contents of these pages are © <sitename> and contributors 2002, 2003.
>
> You may print or download extracts from these pages to a local hard disk for your personal use only provided that none of the text is altered or manipulated. If you recopy the material to individual third parties, we would like you to
>
> acknowledge <sitename> as the source of the material;
>
> and
>
> inform any third parties that these conditions apply to them also.
>
> This site was structured, edited and designed by <names in the team>.

Terms and conditions of use

The issue for writers and web designers here is not what the terms are—lawyers must draft those—but whether people actually read them. Many sites do not allow users to progress through the site unless they have ticked a box to say they have accepted its terms. Where this is of vital importance, it is probably necessary to get a proper signature.

| # Privacy

A good starting point for all research is the British Employment Law portal at <http://www.emplaw.co.uk/>

A privacy statement would include these types of statement, but this is far from definitive. You may need lawyers to draft it for you:

- a commitment to protecting visitors' privacy online;

- to treat any personal information (which means data from which a visitor can be identified, including name, address, email address, and position) that they provide you obtain, in accordance with the provisions of the Data Protection Act of 1998;

- that membership information (where applicable) is only held online for the convenience of all members and that no information is passed to any third parties without permission unless required by law to do so;

- whether or not you use 'cookies', or other forms of information software, to obtain information from visitors to the site and if so why.

Email privacy

There are privacy laws about email—and your company should have a policy on this. If not, it is wise to protect yourself with a sign-off like this:

This email is private and confidential and may be legally privileged. It is intended for recipients only and access by others is unauthorized.

Consider also: confidentiality, liability, and digital signatures.

Web creation resources

The following resources on the Internet may be of help to people doing the whole site themselves.

Technical

- 1st Site Free—create a website in 7 easy steps; good starting point; links to useful tools
  <http://www.1stsitefree.com/>

- Site Aid—freeware HTML editor; looks quite like Microsoft's FrontPage
  <http://www.siteaid.com/>

- FTP Explorer—file transfer software for pc
  <http://www.ftpx.com/>

- Netfinder—file transfer software for Mac
  <http://www.ozemail.com.au/~pli/netfinder>

- The HTML Writers Guild—free membership and access to resources
  <http://www.hwg.org/>

- The CGI Resource Index—scripts that you can buy (some free) e.g. form-handling, guest books, and counters
  <http://www.cgi-resources.com/>

- Web content Accessibility Guidelines
  <http://www.w3.org/tr/wai-webcontent/>

- MSN Messenger Service—one of many easy-access chat room facilities
  <http://msn.co.uk/homepage.asp>

Reference

■ New to the Web—a basic tutorial with a good glossary
<http://home.netscape.com/netcenter/newnet/>

■ Online—a reference guide to using Internet sources
<http://www.smpcollege.com/online-4styles~help>

■ International Standard (ISO 690-2) on citing electronic documents (14 August 2000)
<http://www.nlc-bnc.ca/iso/tc46sc9/standard/690-2e.htm>

■ University of London library notes on citation (5 August 1998)
<http://www.ucl.ac.uk/Library/citing.htm>

■ Acronym Expander—find any web abbreviation or acronym
<http://www.ucc.ie/info/net/acronyms/index.html>

Style

■ Good documents—how to create good business documents for the Internet
<http://www.gooddocuments.com/>

Nielsen, J (2000) Designing Web Usability USA: New Riders Publishing, ISBN 1-56205-810-X

■ Jakob Nielsen's Alert box—fortnightly advice from guru on web usability theory
<http://www.useit.com/alertbox/>

■ Simplified English
<http://www.userlab.com/SE.html>

■ THE SLOT: A Spot for Copy Editors
<http://www.theslot.com/>

■ Times online style guide—useful A–Z
<http://www.thetimes.co.uk/article/0,,14668,00.html>

■ Yale Style Manual
<http://info.med.yale.edu/caim/manual/intro/>

Technical fundamentals

Browsers

A browser is a piece of software that acts as the picture-frame within which all material on the web is viewed. The standard browsers are Netscape, Explorer, and Opera. They work by embedding links into documents using HTML (HyperText Mark-up Language) or XML (eXtensible Mark-up Language). Anything coded in this way can link with any other document anywhere in the world, no matter where it is stored.

The user doesn't see any of this coding but moves through 'pages' of information by clicking a pointer device on a prompt word or hyperlink (traditionally an underlined phrase appearing on-screen in blue). These links are coded instructions to your computer to go and fetch a page from another address.

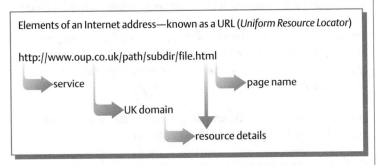

Elements of an Internet address—known as a URL (*Uniform Resource Locator*)

http://www.oup.co.uk/path/subdir/file.html

service

page name

UK domain

resource details

A 'page' can be of variable length; generally half to three printed A4 pages, but it can be 20. The pros and cons of variable page length are detailed on pp. 50–51.

Hyperlinking

A link embedded in the text is the core of hyperlinking—it is exactly like saying, 'Turn to page 100 in the third book on the top shelf of the sixth bookcase in the library of ...' except that the mouse click does it instantly. There is nothing new about hyperlinking except its convenience. The decisions writers need to make about hyperlinking are explored on p. 70.

HTML code

If you want to learn HTML (HyperText Markup Language) the code that tags elements such as text, links, and graphics so that browser software will know how to display a document, then all you really need is a plain text program, like Notepad, and an HTML primer (there are plenty online or buy a book). Look at the source code of pages you like to see how they have been constructed (a right mouse click and select View Source in your browser). If the originators have used JavaScript or Cascading Style Sheets, this may well be more code than you want to know about, so look at simple pages first.

Web creation tools

Standard web creation software 'talks you through' setting up a small site with what are called 'wizards'. These are off-the-peg templates that will produce some linked pages on the basis of answers to standard questions. Graphical HTML editing programs resemble word-processors, and keep the coding hidden from view. This makes it easy for the novice to add links and other features without knowing the codes.

Hard-core web programmers do not use these. They prefer to control the way the code works themselves.

On the whole, writers want to concentrate on the words, not the coding, and as long as it functions, the refinements of the underlying structure are of less importance.

Dynamic documents

Plain HTML documents are static, which means they are in a constant state: a text file that doesn't change. Most people now agree that the future of the web relies on dynamic web pages: ones that respond to them as individuals.

Scripts

Many small programs or routines exist to refine web page functionality, such as automatic form processing, password protection, adding a guest book, and displaying the time or date. The scripts offer some dynamic functions to ordinary HTML-coded pages.

Those who decide to leave scripts to the technically minded need to know is that these scripts sit in a directory on the server called the cgi-bin (CGI stands for Common Gateway Interface).

Popular scripting languages

C
C++
Fortran
PERL
TCL
Any Unix shell
Visual Basic
AppleScript
Java
JavaScript

Database-driven pages

An organisation that has all its basic information in a database can link units to its website by using Active Server Pages (ASP). The text on the page does change because it is being assembled on the fly. The user clicks on a link, and chunks of text are picked up from the database so the page shows a personally tailored collection of items in the database. The underlying coding is dynamic: it can make informed guesses about the information a user will want based on data-gathering about the person.

It is also good for making dates expire automatically (so you don't have to worry about news looking tired).

Database solutions are expensive, and most useful for membership organisations. They are essential for e-commerce.

Uploading to the web

Pages are written and designed on your own computer. When they are ready for the world, you need to transmit them to the service provider's machines. The mechanics of this are frequently opaque even when you are offered a handy button that says 'Publish'.

Most people use a (free) File Transfer Protocol program—FTP for short. If you are technophobic, this may seem frightening at first. But it is really very simple and once you have successfully transferred (or uploaded) your own pages from your computer to the web space on the remote server, you will wonder what the problem was. You will need the following information from your provider: host name; user ID; password.

Metatags

Use metatags if you want your pages to be found easily. Many search routines look for documents based on keywords and descriptions in the 'header' section of the coded page.

> **Metatags for this book might be:**
>
> ```
> <HEAD>
> <META NAME='title' CONTENT=Writing for the Internet>
> <META NAME='description' CONTENT=A language book in the
> One Step Ahead Series>
> <META NAME='keywords' CONTENT=online structure planning
> writing grammar book resources >
> <META NAME='author' CONTENT=Jane Dorner>
> <META NAME='publisher' CONTENT=Oxford University Press>
> </HEAD>
> ```

A metatag is a unit of information that is embedded into the code. Although the user of the web page cannot see the metatag, the machine accessing the code can. It dramatically increases visibility if you write these tags into your web documents.

It is also useful to have an 'author' tag to identify someone in a work group for tracking and for updating purposes.

Glossary

address: Internet locations, commonly called a URL (Uniform Resource Locator). For instance: <http://www.oup.co.uk>. The IP address is expressed in numerals.

ASCII (or plain vanilla text): American Standard Code for Information Interchange. A standard for digital representation of letters, numbers, and control codes; understood by most computers.

ASP: Active Server Pages. Pages created on the fly that pick up information from a database.

bandwidth: a term used to describe how much data you can send through a connection to the Internet. The greater the bandwidth, the faster the rate of data transmission. Lack of bandwidth leads to access problems.

browser: software that allows users to access and navigate the web, commonly Microsoft Explorer, Netscape, and Opera.

Cascading Style Sheets (CSS): style rules that tell the browser how to display all documents in a web—including Braille options.

channel: subject listings on search engines.

click: Mouse- or voice-activated movement that makes something happen on the Internet, like bringing up another page or sending an email.

cookies: bits of identification code that save information about your interaction with a web server on your hard disk so you do not need to type your password or preferences in each time you visit a website.

database: software holding and organizing large amounts of information that can be searched by an Internet user. A storehouse of online information.

dialup: connection to the Internet service provider using a modem and telephone line to access the Internet.

directory: a list of files making up an area of a website.

domain: the part of the Internet address that specifies a computer's location in the world. The address is written as a series of names separated by dots. The most common top-level domains are shown in the box.

domains	
.com	commercial
.ac	education (UK)
.edu	education (US)
.net	network
.gov	public bodies
.pro	professional
.name	individuals
.info	information
.biz	business

download/upload: To download is to transfer a file from the Internet to your own computer. To upload is to send a file to your website.

FAQ: Frequently Asked Questions. Web pages that answer common questions relating to the site.

flame: To send a harsh, critical email message to another user, usually someone who has violated the rules of netiquette.

FTP: File Transfer Protocol. An application program that allows you to move files from your own computer to a server.

hit (also hit rate): the number of individual items on a web page, text, graphics, scripting, and so on. One web page (or pageview) may contain several hits.

home page: the first page a user sees when visiting a website, most commonly applied to personal sites. Also called the 'Splash'.

HTML: Hypertext Markup Language. The programming language of the web, HTML software turns a document into a hyperlinked web page.

HTTP: Hypertext Transfer Protocol. The protocol used to provide hypertext links between pages. It is the standard way of transferring HTML documents between servers and browsers.

hypertext/hyperlink: a highlighted word or graphic in a document that responds to a mouse click to take the user to a related piece of information on the Internet.

Internet: the global network of networks that connects more than 400 million computers throughout the world.

ISP: Internet Service Provider. Any organization that provides access to the Internet.

JavaScript: flashy coding that creates animated and other superior effects.

listserv: email-based mailing lists. Moderated lists are screened before messages are posted to subscribers. Messages to unmoderated lists are automatically forwarded to subscribers.

LIT: (of unknown derivation) the file format used for the Microsoft eReader products.

logon: to sign on to a computer system or password-protected area.

menu: headings (text or graphics buttons) that leads to documents or other subheadings.

Mud and Moo: acronyms (becoming words) for Multi-User Domain (or Dungeon) and Mud Object-Orientated. Virtual spaces on the Internet where people role-play and chat using borrowed identities

netiquette: the rules of conduct for Internet users.

Net-friendly: compatible with the Internet.

newsgroups: bulletin boards of the Internet, grouped round every conceivable subject.

online: when you are logged onto the Internet, you are online.

PDA: Personal Digital Assistant (e.g. Palm Pilot or Psion organizer)

post up: upload a page.

search engine: a program which can trawl through the contents of the web. Used to locate information.

spam: posting the same message to multiple newsgroups

splash: front page of a website, often animated

sticky: in the context of a website, it means having a drawing power so that people will return to the site.

URL: Uniform Resource Locater. Name for the address of any resource on the Internet. You type the URL into your browser, and are taken to that address.

virtual: any computer-generated environment.

virus: malicious and damaging bits of program code. Can arrive in email so vigilance and anti-virus software are required.

Web: Spiderweb-like interconnection of millions of pieces of information located on computers around the world. Web documents use hypertext, which incorporates text and graphical links to other documents and files on Internet-connected computers.

Webmaster: (rarely webmistress) the technical person who oversees the server on which the site is lodged. Can also mean the designer or editor.

WWW: World Wide Web or the web.

XML: eXtensible Markup Language. More sophisticated than HTML as the coding language of the Internet.

If there are any other terms in this book that are unfamiliar, try the What is? site which has definitions of thousands of computer-related words <http/whatis.techtarget.com>

Further reading

Jane Dorner, *The Internet: A Writer's Guide* 2nd edn. (London: A & C Black, 2001), ISBN: 0713661267—looks at a wide range of Internet issues as they concern professional and amateur writers.

Edmond Gillon, ed., *Pictorial Calligraphy and Ornamentation* (New York: Dover, 1972), p. 11.

Constance Hale and Jessie Scanlon, *Wired Style: Principles of English Usage in the Digital Age* (New York: Broadway, 1999), ISBN: 0767903722—a useful house style booklet with a comprehensive A–Z list of digital buzz-words and how to display them onscreen.

Crawford Killian, *Writing for the Web* (Bellingham: Self Counsel Press, 2001), ISBN: 1551803038—advice and practical exercises to help writers break print-based habits with tips on writing for personal and corporate sites.

Amy Jo Kim, *Community Building on the Web* (Berkeley, USA: Peachpit Press, 2000), ISBN: 020 874849—a useful guide for community-based websites, where writing and cheerleading go hand in hand.

Jakob Nielsen, *Designing Web Usability: The Practice of Simplicity*, (Indianapolis: New Riders, 1999), ISBN: 156205810X—an expanded version of the author's Usability AlertBox <http://www.useit.com/alertbox> which is a full and much-consulted resource of readability and web usability research.

David Siegel, *Creating Killer Websites* 2nd edn. (New York: Prentice-Hall 1998), ISBN: 0130813184—a book for designers, very opinionated, but useful for writers who need to be aware of design issues.

Permissions

All websites screenshots appear with the permission of their creators.

Michael Beresford, *Modern English: The User's Guide to Grammar and Style*, (London: Duckworth, 1997), pp. 78–80 reproduced with permission of the publisher.

Index